First World War
and Army of Occupation
War Diary
France, Belgium and Germany

25 DIVISION
Divisional Troops
Royal Army Medical Corps
75 Field Ambulance
25 September 1915 - 15 February 1918

WO95/2239/1

The Naval & Military Press Ltd
www.nmarchive.com
Published in association with The National Archives

Published by

The Naval & Military Press Ltd

Unit 10 Ridgewood Industrial Park,

Uckfield, East Sussex,

TN22 5QE England

Tel: +44 (0) 1825 749494

www.naval-military-press.com

www.nmarchive.com

This diary has been reprinted in facsimile from the original. Any imperfections are inevitably reproduced and the quality may fall short of modern type and cartographic standards.

© Crown Copyright
Images reproduced by permission of The National Archives, London, England, 2015.

Contents

Document type	Place/Title	Date From	Date To
Heading	WO95/2239/1 75 Field Ambulance.		
Heading	75th Fld Ambulance Sep 1915-Feb 1919		
Heading	75th Field Ambulance Vol I Sept 15		
War Diary	Havre	25/09/1915	26/09/1915
War Diary	Lillers	27/09/1915	27/09/1915
War Diary	Le Sart	28/09/1915	29/09/1915
War Diary	Armentieres	30/09/1915	30/09/1915
Heading	25th Division 75th Field Ambulance Vol. 2 Oct 15		
War Diary	Armentieres	01/10/1915	31/10/1915
Heading	25th Division Nov. 15		
War Diary	Armentieres	01/11/1915	30/11/1915
Heading	25th Div		
War Diary	Nieppe	01/12/1915	31/12/1915
Heading	Jan 1916 25th Div		
Heading	War Diary Of 45 Field Ambulance from January 1st-Jan 31st 1916.		
War Diary	Nieppe	01/01/1916	25/01/1916
War Diary	Oultersteene	26/01/1916	31/01/1916
Heading	75th Field Ambulance Feb 1916 March 1916		
War Diary	Uttersteene	01/02/1916	25/03/1916
War Diary	Ecoivres	25/03/1916	30/04/1916
Heading	25th Div No. 75 F. Amb.		
War Diary	Bailleul-aux-cornailles	01/04/1916	19/04/1916
War Diary	Ecoivres	20/04/1916	30/04/1916
Map			
Heading	25th Div No. 75. F. Amb.		
War Diary	Ecoivres	01/05/1916	31/05/1916
Heading	25th Div No. 75 Field Ambulance		
War Diary	Ecoivres	01/06/1916	01/06/1916
War Diary	Bailleul-Aux-Cornailles	02/06/1916	13/06/1916
War Diary	Hericourt	14/06/1916	14/06/1916
War Diary	Noeux	15/06/1916	17/06/1916
War Diary	Epecamps	18/06/1916	18/06/1916
War Diary	Berteaucourt	19/06/1916	24/06/1916
War Diary	Bonneville	25/06/1916	25/06/1916
War Diary	Talmas	27/06/1916	27/06/1916
War Diary	Toutencourt	28/06/1916	30/06/1916
War Diary	Harponville	01/06/1916	01/06/1916
Heading	25th Division 75. Field Ambulance	31/08/1916	31/08/1916
War Diary	Contay	01/07/1916	03/07/1916
War Diary	Bouzincourt	04/07/1916	08/07/1916
War Diary	Millencourt	09/07/1916	17/07/1916
War Diary	Senlis	18/07/1916	18/07/1916
War Diary	Beauval	19/07/1916	19/07/1916
War Diary	Bus-les-Artois	20/07/1916	23/07/1916
War Diary	Sarton	24/07/1916	27/07/1916
War Diary	Vauchelles	28/07/1916	31/07/1916
Heading	Volume X Medical Services 75th Field Ambulance R.A.M.C. July 1916		
Heading	25th Div. 75th Field Ambulance.		

War Diary	Lealvillers	16/08/1916	17/08/1916
War Diary	Map 57.D.W.10.c.9.3.	19/08/1916	21/08/1916
War Diary	W.10.c.9.3	21/08/1916	31/08/1916
Heading	War Diary (Medical) 75th Field Ambulance September 1916		
War Diary	Varennes	01/09/1916	07/09/1916
War Diary	Puchevillers	09/09/1916	09/09/1916
War Diary	Beauval St. Hilaire	10/07/1916	11/07/1916
War Diary	Rederie Farm	12/09/1916	25/09/1916
War Diary	Beauval	26/09/1916	26/09/1916
War Diary	Louvencourt	30/09/1916	30/09/1916
Map			
War Diary	Clairfaye	01/10/1916	02/10/1916
War Diary	Warloy	02/10/1916	23/10/1916
War Diary	Vadencourt Beauval	24/10/1916	30/10/1916
War Diary	Roukloshille	31/10/1916	31/10/1916
Heading	25th Div. 75th Field Ambulance		
War Diary	Nieppe	01/11/1916	25/11/1916
Heading	25th Div. 75th Field Ambulance		
War Diary	Nieppe	02/12/1916	30/12/1916
Map			
Heading	25th Div. 75th Field Ambulance		
War Diary	Nieppe	07/01/1917	28/01/1917
Heading	25th Div.		
War Diary	Nieppe	03/02/1917	20/02/1917
War Diary	Caestre	21/02/1917	21/02/1917
War Diary	Ebblinghem	22/02/1917	22/02/1917
War Diary	Leulinghem	24/02/1917	24/02/1917
Heading	25th Div. 75th Field Ambulance		
War Diary	Leulinghem	03/03/1917	11/03/1917
War Diary	Tattinghem	12/03/1917	17/03/1917
War Diary	Renescure	20/03/1917	20/03/1917
War Diary	Strazeele	21/03/1917	22/03/1917
War Diary	A.18.d.6.2	23/03/1917	24/03/1917
War Diary	A18.d.6.2 Sh.36.	31/03/1917	31/03/1917
Heading	25th Div. 75th. F.a.		
War Diary	A.18.d.6.2 Sh. 36.	02/04/1917	14/04/1917
War Diary	A.18.d.6.2	22/04/1917	30/04/1917
Map			
Heading	25th Div.		
War Diary	A 18.d.6.2. Steenwerck	01/05/1917	19/05/1917
War Diary	A 18.d. 6.2	27/05/1917	30/05/1917
Heading	June 1917 No. 75 F.a.		
War Diary	Ravelsburg	03/06/1917	03/06/1917
War Diary	Ravelsburg	04/06/1917	04/06/1917
War Diary	'K' a.D.S. T.3.d.0.4.	06/06/1917	07/06/1917
War Diary	T.3.d.04	07/06/1917	12/06/1917
War Diary	Bailleul	12/06/1917	21/06/1917
War Diary	Caudescure	23/06/1917	23/06/1917
War Diary	Le Cornet Brassart	24/06/1917	25/06/1917
War Diary	Huninghem	26/06/1917	26/06/1917
War Diary	Lis Burg	26/06/1917	26/06/1917
Heading	July 1917 No. 75. F.a.		
Heading	War Diary Medical 75 F. Ambulance		
War Diary	Lis Burg	08/07/1917	08/07/1917
War Diary	Steenvoorde	09/07/1917	09/07/1917

War Diary	Remy Siding	10/07/1917	24/07/1917
War Diary	Landbouver Farm	25/07/1917	30/07/1917
War Diary	Vansohier Farm	30/07/1917	31/07/1917
Heading	War Diary Medical 75th F. Ambulance 25th Divisional August 1917		
War Diary	Vansohier Farm G21.c.5.7 Sheet 28.	01/08/1917	13/08/1917
War Diary	Vansohier Farm G21.c.5.7	14/08/1917	28/08/1917
War Diary	Vansohier Farm G21.c.5.7 Sh.28	31/08/1917	31/08/1917
Heading	War Diary Medical 75th Field Ambulance R.A.M.C.		
War Diary	Vansohier Farm.	01/09/1917	07/09/1917
War Diary	Waratah Camp D.R.S.	08/09/1917	10/09/1917
War Diary	Caestre	11/09/1917	12/09/1917
War Diary	Thienne	13/09/1917	13/09/1917
War Diary	Auchel	14/09/1917	28/09/1917
Heading	War Diary Medical 75th F. Ambulance October 1917		
War Diary	Auchel C.27.b. 8.3	03/10/1917	04/10/1917
War Diary	Bethune E 5.a.3.0	05/10/1917	05/10/1917
War Diary	Bethune	05/10/1917	31/10/1917
Heading	War Diary Medical 75 F. Ambulance November 1917.		
War Diary	Bethune E 5.a.3.0.	22/11/1917	29/11/1917
Heading	December 1917 75th-Field Ambulance R.A.M.C. War Diary Medical		
War Diary	Bethune Ecole Caterive	01/12/1917	01/12/1917
War Diary	Annezin	02/12/1917	03/12/1917
War Diary	Achiet-Le-Grand	05/12/1917	06/12/1917
War Diary	Favreuil	07/12/1917	12/12/1917
War Diary	Favreuil Camp No 16	12/12/1917	21/12/1917
War Diary	Favreuil	22/12/1917	27/12/1917
Heading	Jan. 1918 No 75. F.a.		
War Diary	Favreuil H.16.d.8.6.	08/01/1918	25/01/1918
Heading	War Diary Medical 75 F. Ambulance		
War Diary	H.16.d.8.6	01/02/1918	12/02/1918
War Diary	Achiet. Le. Grand	13/02/1918	27/02/1918
Heading	March 1918 War Diary Medical 75th Field Ambulance R.A.M.C.		
War Diary	Achiet-Le-Grand Ritz Camp.	03/03/1918	11/03/1918
War Diary	I.27.b.	12/03/1918	12/03/1918
War Diary	I.27.b. Map57.e.	18/03/1918	21/03/1918
War Diary	Beugny	22/03/1918	24/03/1918
War Diary	Miraumont	25/03/1918	25/03/1918
War Diary	Baucourt	25/03/1918	25/03/1918
War Diary	Bertancourt	25/03/1918	26/03/1918
War Diary	Fonquevillers	26/03/1918	26/03/1918
War Diary	Bienvillers	27/03/1918	27/03/1918
War Diary	Puchvillers	28/03/1918	28/03/1918
War Diary	St. Leger	30/03/1918	31/03/1918
Heading	War Diary 75 F. Ambulance R.A.M.C.		
War Diary	Bertaucourt	31/03/1918	01/04/1918
War Diary	Westhof	04/04/1918	11/04/1918
War Diary	A.D.S. Dranoutre Road T.7.d.8.8.	12/04/1918	12/04/1918
War Diary	Croix-de-Poperinghe	13/04/1918	13/04/1918
War Diary	Berthen	14/04/1918	16/04/1918
War Diary	Q.18.b.	16/04/1918	16/04/1918
War Diary	Godewaersvelde	17/04/1918	21/04/1918
War Diary	7.11.a	22/04/1918	25/04/1918
War Diary	Vansohier G.21.c Central Sh. 28.	26/04/1918	29/04/1918

War Diary	Vansohier Farm	30/04/1918	30/04/1918
Heading	War Diary Medical 75th F. Ambulance		
War Diary	Vansohier Farm	01/05/1918	05/05/1918
War Diary	Bellevue Area	07/05/1918	08/05/1918
War Diary	Coulonges	10/05/1918	22/05/1918
War Diary	Igny L'Abbaye	23/05/1918	26/05/1918
War Diary	27th Muscourt	27/05/1918	27/05/1918
War Diary	28th Lagery	28/05/1918	28/05/1918
War Diary	Lagery	28/05/1918	28/05/1918
War Diary	Aougny	29/05/1918	29/05/1918
War Diary	Cuisle	30/05/1918	30/05/1918
War Diary	La Neuville	31/05/1918	31/05/1918
War Diary	Le Shaies	01/05/1918	01/05/1918
Heading	No. 75 F.a.		
War Diary	Les Haies	06/06/1918	18/06/1918
War Diary	Bergeres	18/06/1918	18/06/1918
War Diary	Angluzelles	19/06/1918	21/06/1918
War Diary	St Loup	27/06/1918	27/06/1918
Heading	July 1918 No. 75. F.a.		
War Diary	St Loup	02/07/1918	02/07/1918
War Diary	Gourgancon	03/07/1918	03/07/1918
War Diary	Mailly	04/07/1918	04/07/1918
War Diary	Pontremy	05/07/1918	06/07/1918
War Diary	Torcy	08/07/1918	29/07/1918
Heading	War Diary Medical 75 Field Ambulance		
War Diary	Torcy	11/08/1918	31/08/1918
Heading	September 1918 War Diary Medical 75th Field Ambulance RAMC.		
War Diary	Torcy	01/09/1918	16/09/1918
War Diary	Neuf Moulin	16/09/1918	25/09/1918
War Diary	Buire	27/09/1918	28/09/1918
War Diary	Maricourt	29/09/1918	29/09/1918
Heading	War Diary Medical Services 75th Field Ambulance October 1918		
War Diary	Moislains	01/10/1918	07/10/1918
War Diary	Railway Trench Grandcourt	08/10/1918	11/10/1918
War Diary	Honnechy	12/10/1918	23/10/1918
War Diary	Le Cateau	24/10/1918	31/10/1918
Heading	War Diary Medical Services 75th Field Ambulance November 1918		
War Diary	Lecateau	04/11/1918	04/11/1918
War Diary	Landrecies	05/11/1918	05/11/1918
War Diary	Boursies	08/11/1918	12/11/1918
War Diary	Lecateau	13/11/1918	30/11/1918
Heading	War Diary Medical Services 75th Field Ambulance December 1918		
War Diary	Sthilairi	01/12/1918	08/12/1918
War Diary	Avesnes Lez Aubert	09/12/1918	09/12/1918
War Diary	Avesnes Les Aubert	10/12/1918	31/12/1918
Heading	War Diary Medical Services 75th Field Ambulance January 1919		
War Diary	Avesnes Les Aubert	01/01/1919	31/01/1919
Heading	War Diary 75th Field Ambulance Medical February 1919		
War Diary	Avesnes Les Aubert	01/02/1918	15/02/1918

WO 195/2239

/1 75 Field Ambulance.

25TH DIVISION
MEDICAL

75TH FLD AMBULANCE
SEP 1915 - FEB 1919

25/K Division

1699/71

75th Field Ambulance
Vol I
Sept. 15

Sept '15
/
Dec '18

WAR DIARY
or
INTELLIGENCE SUMMARY.

(Erase heading not required.)

75th Field Ambulance
Army Form C. 2118

Instructions regarding War Diaries and Intelligence Summaries are contained in F. S. Regs., Part II. and the Staff Manual respectively. Title pages will be prepared in manuscript.

Place	Date	Hour	Summary of Events and Information	Remarks and references to Appendices
Havre	25/9/15	7am	Disembarked from T.S. "Ballarghan" 4 Officers 65 Other ranks 62 Horses & 2 Travelling Kitchens	
			From T.S. "Queen Alexandra" 10 Officers (4 Chaplains attached) 162 Other ranks	
		1pm	Reached No 5 Rest Camp & received orders to entrain at Gare des Marchandises at 1.30 a.m.	
	26/9/15	12.30am	Marches from No 5 Rest Camp to Station in bright moonlight night. Accompanied by two platoons S.W. Borderers (Pioneers) & with regimental transport.	
			Loaded by 3.30 a.m. delay due to shunting waggons.	
Lillers	27/9/15	1.45pm	Reached Lillers, unloaded transport & received orders to proceed to billets at Lorgnehen village.	
			Somehow to billets at le Sart - via Rieux	
Sart	28/9/15	9am	Marches from Lorgnehen - reached Farm du Roi Paris at 3.45pm. St Venant. Received orders from 7th Brigade to march on 29th via Morville to Merris.	

H.T. Davidson
Major RAMC

Army Form C. 2118

WAR DIARY
or
INTELLIGENCE SUMMARY.
(Erase heading not required.)

Instructions regarding War Diaries and Intelligence Summaries are contained in F. S. Regs., Part II. and the Staff Manual respectively. Title pages will be prepared in manuscript.

Place	Date	Hour	Summary of Events and Information	Remarks and references to Appendices
L. Cart	29/9/15	6:30am	Received orders from 74th Brigade to proceed by nearest route to Armentieres & report to A.D.M.S, 2.5th Division at Nieppe.	
		4 Am	Reported & took over building, Ecole, Rue Messines as a dressing Station.	
Armentieres	30/9/15	9am	Opened one Section of this Field Ambulance to treat sick from the 74th Brigade. Visited Advanced dressing stations. Regimental aidpost and trenches of 3.0th Division for instruction.	

H A Davidson
Major R.A.M.C
O C 7 th F.A. Ams?

51/7431

35th Division

75th Field Ambulance
Vol: 2

Oct 15.

Cerias

Army Form C. 2118.

WAR DIARY
or
INTELLIGENCE SUMMARY.
(Erase heading not required.)

Instructions regarding War Diaries and Intelligence Summaries are contained in F. S. Regs., Part II. and the Staff Manual respectively. Title pages will be prepared in manuscript.

Place	Date	Hour	Summary of Events and Information	Remarks and references to Appendices
Armentières	1 10/15	1 p.m.	A few medical cases admitted from units of 25th Division & evacuated by Convoy to Clearing Hospital at Bailleul.	
"	2 10/15	11 a.m.	Three Officers, 3 N.C.O.s & 20 men attached to 2nd Northumbrian Field Ambulance for instruction. One Medical Officer admitted to the Ambulance from the 11th Lancashire Fusiliers and an officer from the Field Ambulance sent to take his place.	
"	3 10/15	4 p.m.	Received orders from the A.D.M.S. 25th Division to relieve the 1st Northumbrian Fd. Amb. from the night of the 3/4th Oct.	
"	4 10/15		At this post the Regimental aid post is used as an advanced dressing station, it is situated beside the Communication trench in a house where there are cellars for shelter in case of shell fire.	

2353 Wt. W2514/1454 700,000 5/15 D. D. & L. A.D.S.S./Forms/C. 2118.

Army Form C. 2118.

WAR DIARY
or
INTELLIGENCE SUMMARY. 75th Field Ambulance
(Erase heading not required.)

Instructions regarding War Diaries and Intelligence Summaries are contained in F.S. Regs., Part II. and the Staff Manual respectively. Title pages will be prepared in manuscript.

Place	Date	Hour	Summary of Events and Information	Remarks and references to Appendices
Armentières	4/10/15		The Aid post is at Map 36. C 9 d 9.6. The personnel consist of One Officer, 1 Sergeant, fifteen bearers, with Medical Comforts, Surgical Haversack, Shell dressings, Blankets, waterproof sheets, Medical Comforts. Motor Ambulance transport has to evacuate casualties.	yes
	5/10/15	8.30am	Casualties brought to Casualty Clearing Station. Lieut. S.C.W. White 13th Cheshire Regt. Bullet wound abdomen. One man Bullet wound knee joint.	yes / yes
	6/10/15	6pm	No casualties beyond the ordinary sick. Evacuated 3 men to D.R.S. & 1 to C.C.S.	no
	7/10/15	6pm	Two casualties slight from 13th Cheshires. Evacuated 3 cases to D.R.S. & 4 to C.C.S.	
	8/10/15	9.30am	The 75th Field Ambulance took over the advanced dressing station and the collection of wounded from three additional aid posts.	yes

WAR DIARY
or
INTELLIGENCE SUMMARY. J.J.K Field Amb

Army Form C. 2118.

Place	Date	Hour	Summary of Events and Information	Remarks and references to Appendices
Armentiers	8/10/15		The advanced dressing station is at Map 36, C1.d	
			aid posts " " C3.b No 1 post -	
			" " 28 U27.b " 2 "	
			" " U20.d " 3 "	
			The personnel for the advanced dressing station is as follows:	
			Officers other ranks Team Dublin. Moto Ambulance Drivers Waggon orderly	
			2 Inst. Dublin. 30 2 1	
			5	
			The Bearers are distributed as follows:—	
			No 1 post - 4 ; No 2 post - 4 ; No 3 post - 2,	
			The remainder are held in reserve and to relieve the men	
			in the aid posts every 24 hours.	
			Equipment of advanced dressing station:—	
			One water cart, medical store limber, One Ambulance Waggon,	
			Stretchers, Blankets, Waterproof sheets, Med. Comfort panier,	
			motor Ambulance brought in charge of an officer calls	
			Three a day or oftener if necessary, at the advanced	
			dressing station to remove casualties to the main dressing station	

Army Form C. 2118.

WAR DIARY
or
INTELLIGENCE SUMMARY. 75 th "N" Field Amb"
(Erase heading not required.)

Instructions regarding War Diaries and Intelligence Summaries are contained in F.S. Regs., Part II. and the Staff Manual respectively. Title pages will be prepared in manuscript.

Place	Date	Hour	Summary of Events and Information	Remarks and references to Appendices
Armentieres	8/10/15	6.30 p.m.	Casualties:— Lieut. V./t Kempson 11th Lancs. Fus. Concussion heat & concussion. 1 man " " " Wounded Chest (Shell) Evacuated 3 to D.R.S. & 5 to C.C.S.	
"	9/10/15	"	Casualties 1 man wounded 8th S. Lancs S. Evacuated sick + wounded to D.R.S. 5 C.C.S. 1 Duty 2	
"	10/10/15	"	" D.R.S. 10 C.C.S. 2 Duty 1	
"	11/10/15	"	Wounded admitted 1 N.C.O. 3 men. D.R.S. 8 Sick transfers evacuated to " C.C.S. 2 " duty 8	

Army Form C. 2118.

WAR DIARY
or
INTELLIGENCE SUMMARY. 75th Fld. Ambce.
(Erase heading not required.)

Instructions regarding War Diaries and Intelligence Summaries are contained in F.S. Regs., Part II. and the Staff Manual respectively. Title pages will be prepared in manuscript.

Place	Date	Hour	Summary of Events and Information	Remarks and references to Appendices
Armentières	12/10/15	6.30 p.m.	Three wounded N.C.O's + men admitted to the Field Ambulance. Evacuated to D.R.S 4, C.C.S 1, duty 1. The Field Ambulance personnel are now distributed as follows. Casualties are taken from 4 Regimental aid posts, at each of which there are 4 bearers from the Field Ambulance & one pool has an N.C.O in addition. At the advanced dressing station are two Officers + the bearers of one section of the Field Ambulance with an N.C.O & four men of the tent-subdivision, the men for stretcher of the aid posts are supplied from the advanced dressing station. In addition there are two motor drivers, one waggon orderly, one A.S.C. driver. The remainder of the personnel is at the main dressing station, which supplies the N.C.O & bearers for the fourth aid post.	

WAR DIARY
or
INTELLIGENCE SUMMARY. 70th Field Ambulance

Army Form C. 2118.

(Erase heading not required.)

Place	Date	Hour	Summary of Events and Information	Remarks and references to Appendices
Armentières	13/10/15	6.30 p.m	Number of Casualties 3 men wounded. Cases evacuated to D.T.S. 6, C.C.S. 5 (includes this case of measles) duty - 13 1/A.D.	
"	14/10/15	"	Number of Casualties 3 men wounded. Cases evacuated to D.R.S. 1, C.C.S. 6, duty 6 1/A.D.	
"	15/10/15	"	Personnel — 1 N.C.O. + 10 men sent to the baths for troops, for temporary duty. Casualties — 2 men wounded. Cases evacuated to D.R.S. 2, C.C.S. 3, duty 6 1/A.D.	

Army Form C. 2118.

WAR DIARY
or
INTELLIGENCE SUMMARY. 75th Field Ambulance

(Erase heading not required.)

Place	Date	Hour	Summary of Events and Information	Remarks and references to Appendices
ARMENTIERES	16/2	1630	One wounded man admitted. Evacuated to D.R.S. 3 C.C.S. 3 July 2 KAD	
"	17/2/15		No wounded admitted. Evacuated to D.R.S. 1 Officer 1 man. July 7 3 men. KAD	
"	18/10/15		Selected a house in Rue de Strasbourg hospital for Officers, it could take 10 patients. KAD. 10 wounded N.C.O's & men admitted, most of the wounds severe head & abdomen, one man died on the way to the C.C.S. Evacuated to D.R.S. 3 C.C.S. 8 July 4 KAD.	

2353 Wt. W2544/1454 700,000 5/15 D. D. & L. A.D.S.S./Forms/C. 2118.

WAR DIARY
or
INTELLIGENCE SUMMARY 75th Fd. Amb/oc

Army Form C. 2118.

(Erase heading not required.)

Place	Date	Hour	Summary of Events and Information	Remarks and references to Appendices
ARMENTIERES	19/3	6.40 pm	10 N.C.O's & men were admitted with wounds.	
			Cases of wounded sick evacuated to :- D.R.S. — 7	
			C.C.S. — 11	
			duty — 1.	
			One sick Officer admitted to Officer's Hospital	
	20/15	7 pm	One Officer, 1 N.C.O & 18 men arrived from the 77th Field Ambulance for a course of instruction in dressing Station routine.	HRD
				HRD
"	21st		Captain S.W.H. McCulloch 8th Borderers wounded (Gunshot wounds leg/ fracture)	
			N.C.O's & men wounded 5.	
			Cases of sick & wounded evacuated — D.R.S 10	
			C.C.S 2	
			duty 1	HRD
"	22nd		Two cases of wounds admitted & six cases sick & wounded evacuated	HRD
			10 cases discharges to duty.	
"	23rd		One case of wounds admitted; 13 cases sick & wounded evacuated	HRD
			" " " " 3 "	HRD
			" " " " 4 "	HRD

Army Form C. 2118.

WAR DIARY
or
INTELLIGENCE SUMMARY. 75th Field Amb RC

(Erase heading not required.)

Instructions regarding War Diaries and Intelligence
Summaries are contained in F.S. Regs., Part II.
and the Staff Manual respectively. Title pages
will be prepared in manuscript.

Place	Date	Hour	Summary of Events and Information	Remarks and references to Appendices
ARMENTIERES	24/4/15	7 pm	6 cases of wounds admitted.	
			+ sick evacuated.	
	25 "	12 "	No 3 Regt. Aid Post: Paris de Plogsteert collected & wounded from this aid post – has been handed over to No 76th Field Amb. We are getting 75th Fld Amb to move wounds on the north by the La Panarin Plogsteert Road for the South by the Ruin Lys.	map
	"	"	3 cases of wounds admitted.	
	"	"	+ sick evacuated.	
	26 "	"	One Officer, 20 NCO's men of 77th Fld Amb arrived for instruction in dressing station duties	
	"	"	3 Cases of wounds admitted	
	27 "	"	+ sick evacuated	
	28 "	"	24 cases of sick evacuated, no wounds admitted	map
	29 "	"	1 Case of wounds admitted, 18 Cases sick evacuated	map
	30 "	"	6 cases of wounds " " 20 cases " "	map
	31 "	"	4 " " " 24 " "	map
	"	"	4 " " " 17 " "	map

2353 Wt. W2511/1454 700,000 5/15 D. D. & L. A.D.S.S./Form/C. 2118.

75 7/8 7 C.
vol. 3

131/7654

amt

25/11 Kraun

Nov 1915

Nov. 15.

Army Form C. 2118

WAR DIARY
or
INTELLIGENCE SUMMARY. 73rd (1st W.) Field Ambulance.

(Erase heading not required.)

Instructions regarding War Diaries and Intelligence Summaries are contained in F. S. Regs., Part II. and the Staff Manual respectively. Title pages will be prepared in manuscript.

Place	Date	Hour	Summary of Events and Information	Remarks and references to Appendices
ARMENTIERES	1/7/15	7 pm	In addition to the conveyance a day to the A.D.S, one motor ambulance waggon calls at the Reserve Billets at 10 am to collect sick. Three wheeled carriages for stretcher have been received & one has been sent from the unit of each aid post. Received notice from the A.D.M.S. that the Divisional Rest Station was full & that patients should be kept + treated as far as possible in the Ambulance for the present. Cases admitted 20 (1 wounded); cases evacuated & discharged twenty 29.	
"	2nd "	"	" 21 (2 "); " " " " 6.	
"	"	"	The weather has been very had lately, continuous rain & several casualties have occurred owing to dug outs & trenches giving way.	
"	3rd "	"	Cases admitted 20 (2 wounded); cases evacuated & discharged to duty 12. Remaining in hospital 64 including 5 officers in consequent - home.	
"	4th "	"	Cases admitted 21 (1 officer) 43 men wounded; cases evacuated & discharged thirty 26. Most of the dug outs used by the stretcher bearers in the trenches were flooded out; one of the Regt' aid posts had to be closed & the remainder are to be refined temporarily. The system of evacuation from aid posts has worked very well as far. The wheeled stretchers have been of great assistance. One motor ambulance car was slightly damaged by running into a tree at night, the cart was standing on the wrong side of the road.	
"	5th "	"	25 cases admitted (1 officer, 7 men wounded); cases evacuated & discharged today 18.	

WAR DIARY
or
INTELLIGENCE SUMMARY. 75th Fld. Amb.

Army Form C. 2118

Place	Date	Hour	Summary of Events and Information	Remarks and references to Appendices
ARMENTIERES	6th	7 pm	23 cases admitted to Hospital; 17 cases evacuated & discharged to duty. 11 Cases of Trench feet have been admitted from the 13th Cheshire Regt. The trenches were very wet, the men had been standing & working in water, none of the men has seen the Ant: frost bite powder before going into the trenches, but (-) they had dry socks to change. None of the cases were severe, the feet were red & very sore & in cases swollen with tingling sensation & have ? sensation in the toes. They all recovered after little more than 24 hrs rest & treat-ment, which mainly consisted of baths & warm dressings.	
"	7th	"	17 cases admitted to Hospital; 10 cases evacuated & discharged to duty.	
"	8th	"	36 " " " " " (7 wounded); 42 cases evacuated & discharged to duty. Cases remaining in Hospital 8 Officers 74 N.C.O.S & men. The position of the Regt. Aid posts which are evacuated by the 75th Fld Amb. are now as follows:- Map 36, C.9, d 9.5. " C.3; d 4.6. " 28 U.27, b.	
"	9th	"	The area to the north is taken over by the 76th Fld. Amb. & the line south of the 63 Fld. Amb. 24 cases admitted to Hospital (3 wounded); 29 cases evacuated & discharged to duty; 8 cases " " " (2 wounded); 13 discharged to duty & evacuated.	
"	10th	"		

WAR DIARY
or
INTELLIGENCE SUMMARY. 75th W. Fld. Amb.

(Erase heading not required.)

Army Form C. 2118

Instructions regarding War Diaries and Intelligence Summaries are contained in F.S. Regs., Part II. and the Staff Manual respectively. Title pages will be prepared in manuscript.

Place	Date	Hour	Summary of Events and Information	Remarks and references to Appendices
ARMENTIERES	11/5	7pm	15 cases admitted to Hospital (3 wounded); 26 cases evacuated & discharged to duty. Two Douglas Motor Cycles have been received, making the regular 8 motor cycles with the Ambulance up to three; one cycle has been stationed at the A.D. Station.	1720.
"	13/5	11am	Cases admitted on 12th 32 (18 wounded); 22 Cases evacuated & discharged to duty. There was a bombardment of this town about 9.45pm on the 12th. 17 of the wounded were sent up in this dressing station, they belonged to the 21st Division. Cases admitted on 13th 19 (1 wounded); 30 cases evacuated & discharged to duty.	1720.
"	14/5	7pm	11 Cases admitted to Hospital (1 wounded); 15 cases discharged to duty.	1720.
"	15"	"	12 " " " " " (2) " " " " " " 3, 15	1700
"	16"	"	Yesterday one riding horse was missing, with saddle & bridle & equipment while at exercise, the R. Prov. 25th + 21st Div. have been notified to notice with description put in D.R.O.'s. 21 Cases admitted to Hospital (1 Officer + 6 men wounded), 20 cases evacuated & discharged to duty. The horse was returned yesterday; it had been taken to lines of 21st Div.	
"	17"	"	15 cases admitted to Hosp. (6 wounded); 19 Cases evacuated & discharged to duty. Several shells fell in the vicinity of this Hospital & various wounded & cases fell in their dressing station.	

WAR DIARY
or
INTELLIGENCE SUMMARY. 75th W. Fld. Amb.

(Erase heading not required.)

Army Form C. 2118

Instructions regarding War Diaries and Intelligence Summaries are contained in F.S. Regs., Part II. and the Staff Manual respectively. Title pages will be prepared in manuscript.

Place	Date	Hour	Summary of Events and Information	Remarks and references to Appendices
ARMENTIERES	18th	7pm	The town was shelled yesterday for over three hours & so again till nearly 1pm now. There was a good deal of damage done but only 4 casualties amongst the troops seemed in the 1st – 9th – were near the Rue Bayard. In the Rue de Dunkirk the Officers considered I have now struck by 3 shells & pretty badly wrecked. There were 5 patients left – all but 1 had injury, the [word] great part the gas work of the R.A.M.C. Corporal in charge who [word] there all tended safe cases in time. I consider the behaviour of No 32275 Cpl. Baldwin A.R. was most creditable in very trying conditions & that his action & coolness tended to help probably saves several lives. 15 cases admitted to Hospital (8 wounded); 22 cases one acute or discharge & these (1 no)	
"	19th	"	19 cases admitted to Hospital (6 wounded); 46 " "	
"	20th	"	Leaving 22 cases in the Hospital, in case of further bombardment these could be evacuated quickly by own horse Motor Ambulances.	
"	"	"	13 cases admitted to Hospital (3 wounded). The evacuation or discharges to duty. A small station disinfector has been built in the dressing station & that will Vic Kill & destroy patients verbal infectious germs, in Vie Dresh disinfector is only available twice a week. Soup Kitchen (been kept open) have been opened at the A.D. station at the Regl. Aid Posts under the supervision of the 75th. Fd. Amb. &c.	
"	21st	"	12 admissions to Hospital; 7 evacuated & discharged to duty.	
"	22nd	"	18 " " " " (4 wounded); 7 evacuated or discharged to duty.	

2353 Wt. W2514/1454 700,000 5/15 D.D.& L. A.B.S.S./Forms/C. 2118.

Army Form C. 2118

WAR DIARY
or
INTELLIGENCE SUMMARY.   75th Fld. Ambulance.
(Erase heading not required.)

Instructions regarding War Diaries and Intelligence Summaries are contained in F. S. Regs., Part II. and the Staff Manual respectively. Title pages will be prepared in manuscript.

Place	Date	Hour	Summary of Events and Information	Remarks and references to Appendices
ARMENTIERES	23/6/15	7 p.m.	14 cases admitted to Hospital (2 wounded); 17 cases evacuated or discharged to duty. It has been decided to remove the Dressing Station from ARMENTIERES to NIEPPE so as to have it in the 25th Div. Area instead of in the 12th Div. area as at present.	
	24th	"	7 cases admitted to Hospital (3 wounded); 17 cases evacuated or discharged to duty	
	25th	"	17 " " " " (2 "); 18 " " " "	
	26th	"	18 " " " " (4 "); 13 " " " "	
	27th	"	12 " " " " ; 27 " " " "	
			The Dressing Station was changed today to the Square NIEPPE; ARMENTIERES was shelled this morning several of them near the Dressing Station, only one man was treated for injuries due to Shrapnell.	
	28th	"	17 cases admitted to Hospital (10 officers 111 men wounded); 13 evacuated or discharged to duty. The M.O. 2 R.I. Rifles Lieut. McKenzie was killed this morning while dressing a case; Lieut. Burrows R.A.M.C. who was attached to this Field Ambulance was sent to take his place.	
	29th	"	18 patients admitted to Hosp (1 wounded); 13 evacuated or discharged to duty.	
	30th	"	12 " " " " ; 5 " " " "	

75ř Z.a.
hod. 4

131
/784

25 h Kn

Dec. 1915

WAR DIARY

75th 1/1st Fd. Amb.

Army Form C. 2118.

INTELLIGENCE SUMMARY.
(Erase heading not required.)

Place	Date	Hour	Summary of Events and Information	Remarks and references to Appendices
NIEPPE	1st Sep.	7 pm	20 Cases admitted to the Dressing Station (2 wounded); 17 cases evacuated or returned to duty. 5 men arrived from the Base as a reinforcement; have been billeted on the strength. Zinc roofs of huts have been completed for patients.	
	2nd "		12 Cases admitted (1 wounded); 17 cases evacuated or returned to duty.	
	3rd "		30 " " (3 wounded); 22 " " " "	
	" "		French 90 men down in by a mine last evening & even of horses & men was admitted during the night, no serious wounds.	
	4th "		52 cases admitted (15 wounded); 38 cases discharged to duty or evacuated. One heavy draft here was severely injured in the horse lines, most the chest the injury was due to an accident - the horses falling & getting tied up in his head ropes.	
	5th "		10 men admitted to the Dressing Station (3 wounded); 14 evacuated or discharged to duty	
	6th "		33 " " " (2 Officers, 10 men wounded); 15 evacuated or discharged to duty. The wounded Officers included Lieut. _____ Scott R.A.M.C. att. 1/1st Lancs. Fus. & has been replaced by Lieut. Pink R.A.M.C. from the 75th Fd. Amb. etc.	
	7th "		20 cases admitted (2 wounded), 29 evacuated or discharged to duty.	
	8th "		16 " " (1 Officer + 3 men wounded); 19 " " " "	
	9th "		13 " " (2 wounded); 11 " " " "	
	" "		Nieppe was shelled again yesterday; only one case of slight wound occurred; two Guns were sent into Armentières which regularly 9th Brigade Hd. Qrs. to give covering.	
	10th "		16 cases admitted (1 Officer + 3 men wounded). 20 evacuated or discharged. Several shells again came over + burst in the vicinity. The H.Q of	
	11th "		2.3. " admitted " " " " ; 16 evacuated or discharged to duty.	

WAR DIARY or INTELLIGENCE SUMMARY

Army Form C. 2118.

/5th F.A. Amb/

Place	Date	Hour	Summary of Events and Information	Remarks and references to Appendices
NIEPPE	12 Dec	7pm	15 cases admitted (3 wounded); 19 evacuated or discharged to duty. One section of the Field Ambce is kept ready to move in case of emergency, in case this Dressing Station was suddenly knocked out by shell fire; a point has been fixed on the Papot-STEENWERCK road where a temporary dressing station could be made.	
"	13th	"	17 cases admitted (4 wounded); 16 evacuated or discharged to duty. NIEPPE was again shelled yesterday. Several casualties amongst the civilians & small soldiers slightly wounded; a shell struck the house next to the Officers' mess of this Ambulance - Lieut Hughes - Capt. Rennie & our orderly had slight cuts but were all fit to resume duty.	
"	14th	"	21 cases admitted (2 wounded); 16 evacuates or discharges to duty	
"	15th	"	16 " " (2 "); 23 "	
"	16th	"	19 " " (5 "); 23 "	
"	17th	"	10 " " ; 21 "	
"	18th	"	23 " " (3 wounded); 4 "	
"	19th	"	25 " " (9 wounded); 35 "	
			One 6" shell struck a house in Nieppe today, it went thro' & exploded inside the cottage where there were 5 people, only one was slightly injured.	
"	20th	"	13 cases admitted (2 wounded); 23 cases evacuated or discharged to duty.	
"	21st	"	13 " " (4 "); 8 "	
			Three Officers on same steamer leave (8 days) each week from today. Field Ambulances are asked to arrange transport when favourable.	

Army Form C. 2118.

WAR DIARY
or
INTELLIGENCE SUMMARY. 75th Field Ambulance.
(Erase heading not required.)

Instructions regarding War Diaries and Intelligence
Summaries are contained in F.S. Regs., Part II.
and the Staff Manual respectively. Title pages
will be prepared in manuscript.

Place	Date	Hour	Summary of Events and Information	Remarks and references to Appendices
NIEPPE	22nd	7 p.m.	15 cases admitted (2 wounded); 10 evacuated on discharged to duty.	
"	23rd	"	14 " " " " " 16 " " "	
"	"	"	One M.O. sent from this unit for temporary duty with the 8th W.L.N.L.	
"	24th	"	17 cases admitted (4 wounded); 19 evacuated or discharged to duty	
"	25th	"	11 " " (2 ") ; 9 " " "	
"	26th	"	15 " " (4 ") ; 10 " " "	
"	27th	"	25 " " (4 ") ; 25 " " "	
"	28th	"	25 " " (2 ") ; 21 " " "	
"	29th	"	41 " " (one officer + 22 men wounded); 40 " " "	
"	"	"	The wounded were from two battalions that carried out bombing attacks. The greater proportion of the wounds were not of a serious nature.	
"	30 "	"	18 cases admitted (1 officer + 3 men wounded); 13 evacuated or discharged to duty	
"	31 "	"	19 " " (1 wounded); 15 discharged to duty or evacuated	

M A Davidson
Major RAMC
O.C. 75th F.A.

Jan 1916

F/1/2/11

25th Bn

75th F.A.
Vol: 5

75 FA

5

Confidential

War Diary
of
75 Field Ambulance

from January 1st — Jan 31st 1916

Despatched 2.2.16.

J Stephens
Capt RAMC (LR)
for O/C 75 F.A.

WAR DIARY or INTELLIGENCE SUMMARY

Army Form C. 2118.

Place	Date	Hour	Summary of Events and Information	Remarks and references to Appendices
NIEPPE	1/1/16	7 pm	13 patients admitted to Advanced Dressing Station (no wounded); 11 evacuated to discharged to duty	man
"	2nd	"	18 " " " (3 "); 25 "	man
"	3rd	"	38 "	man
"	4	"	23 " " " (1 officer 6 men wounded); 36 "	(man)
"	5	"	15 " " " (2 wounded) ; 23 "	(man)
"	6	"	15 " " " (1 officer 5 men) ; 17 "	man
"	7	"	26 " " " (4 wounded) ; 26 "	man
"	8	"	17 " " " (1 wounded) ; 20 "	man
"	9	"	A few shells fell in men quarters, one civilian was hurt & kept in hospital 15" cases admitted (4 wounded); 11 evacuated or discharged to duty	man
"	10	"	31 " " " (4 ") ; 33 "	man
"	11	"	24 " " " (7 ") ; 22 "	man
"	12	"	15 " " " (2 ") ; 18 "	man
"	13	"	12 " " " (3 ") ; 18 "	man
"	14	"	19 " " " (4 ") ; 17 "	man
"	15	"	21 " " " (5 ") ; 21 "	man
"	16	"	17 " " " (4 ") ; 17 "	man
"	17	"	22 " " " (3 ") ; 9 "	man
"	18	"	13 " " " (1 ") ; 9.8 "	man
"	19	"	10.2 " " " (officers 75 men) ; 28 "	man
"	20	"	13 " " " (2 men wounded) ; 17 "	man
"	21	"	18 " " " (6 ")	man

Army Form C. 2118.

WAR DIARY
or
INTELLIGENCE SUMMARY.
(Erase heading not required.)

Instructions regarding War Diaries and Intelligence Summaries are contained in F. S. Regs., Part II. and the Staff Manual respectively. Title pages will be prepared in manuscript.

Place	Date	Hour	Summary of Events and Information	Remarks and references to Appendices
NIEPPE			Summary of Routine of Evacuation of Sick & Wounded by 75th Field Ambulance. The area evacuated extends from the River LYS where it joins the HOUPLINES & ARMENTIERES to the South, and up to the PLOEGSTEERT, TOUQUET, BERTHE road on the North. The Regimental Aid posts are situated at map 36 C.9; 4.4.6. C.3; d.4.6. 28 b.27, b 30 C.1. d. The advanced dressing stations are situated at 2 Officers & 2 other ranks. personnel 2 Officers 42 other ranks. equipment One pair of Thresh's Pannier, drawings, disinfectants, apparatus for A.T. Serum, Oxygen cylinders, ammonia cycles, stoves &c. one motor Ambulance waggon, one limber, one water cart, one bearer stretcher, four wheeled stretcher carriers. The A. D. Station party send 4 bearers to each Reg'l Aid post when they report for 24 hours, the wounded are brought down on the stretcher railways & then by wheeled stretcher to the A. D. Station. There are extra motor Ambulance calls twice a day at the A.D.S the waggons billets to collect sick + wounded, they can calls in the evening relieve the car at the A.D.S. The personnel at the A.D.S. do duty for one week, when they are relieved by the next section for duty. Horse Ambulance waggons leave the main dressing station for the D.T. Station daily at 9 a.m., C.C.S. & and go by the Motor Convoy at 2.30 p.m. A map is attached showing the positions of the various posts and the roads of the Ambulances on either flank.	

2353 Wt. W3H/1454 700,000 5/15 D. D. & L. A.D.S.S./Form/C. 2118.

Army Form C. 2118.

WAR DIARY
or
INTELLIGENCE SUMMARY. 75 ᵗʰᶜ F.A.

(Erase heading not required.)

Instructions regarding War Diaries and Intelligence
Summaries are contained in F. S. Regs., Part II.
and the Staff Manual respectively. Title pages
will be prepared in manuscript.

Place	Date	Hour	Summary of Events and Information	Remarks and references to Appendices
NIEPPE	22ⁿᵈ Jan.	from	20 cases admitted (2 wounded); 13 cases evacuated or discharged to duty.	1/1/5840
"	23ʳᵈ	"	10 " " (" "); 21 " " " " " " "	17.20
"	"	"	An advance party of two Officers + 30 O. Ranks arrived from 29ᵗʰ F.A. to take over this dressing station. the A.D.Station in Plougstert. Sent two advance parties, (each consisting of One Officer + 15 other ranks R.A.M.C., two other ranks A.S.C., one Officer + 15 other ranks R.A.M.C., two officers riding horses + limber with medical stores) to take over the dressing stations at LA CRECHE Map 36 A.5.d.8.8. + OULTERSTEENE F.9.a.4.4.	
"	24ᵗʰ	"	25 cases admitted (3 wounded); 33 men evacuated or discharged to duty.	17.20
"	25ᵗʰ	"	9 " " (" "); 30 " " " " " " "	17.20
OULTERSTEENE	26ᵗʰ	"	3 " " " " " " " " " " " "	17.20
"	"	"	Lt.- NIEPPE 10 a.m. + marches to OULTERSTEENE that 36 A.F. F.a.4.4. to rest + refit. A small dressing station has been formed at the above point + another at LA CRECHE sheet 36 A.5.d.8.8.	Strength on Lieut. Fitzhugh Locke (R.F Army Reserve) joined S.O. on
"	27ᵗʰ	"	11 cases admitted (no wounded); 8 cases evacuated or discharged to duty (include OULTERSTEENE + LA CRECHE dressing station)	M
"	28ᵗʰ	"	3 cases admitted (no wounded); 11 cases evacuated or discharged to duty	M
"	29ᵗʰ	"	14 cases admitted (no wounded); 13 cases evacuated or discharged to duty	M

Army Form C. 2118.

WAR DIARY
or
INTELLIGENCE SUMMARY. 75th F.A.

(Erase heading not required.)

Place	Date	Hour	Summary of Events and Information	Remarks and references to Appendices
TOTTERSTEENE	30 Jan	9 pm	9 cases admitted (no wounded); 10 discharged duty or evacuated	
"	31 "	"	15 cases admitted (10 wounded); 14 discharged duty or evacuated. The ambulance at Poel being station keeping very limited my myself can are retained so not being evacuated within 24 hours to D.R.S. or C.C.S.	

J. Stephenson Capt. R.A.M.C.(L.R.)
for Lt. Col.
Comdg 75 F.A.
(on leave)

45th Field Ambulance

S
Feb 1916
Mar "

WAR DIARY
or
INTELLIGENCE SUMMARY.
(Erase heading not required.)

Army Form C. 2118.

Instructions regarding War Diaries and Intelligence Summaries are contained in F.S. Regs., Part II. and the Staff Manual respectively. Title pages will be prepared in manuscript.

Place	Date	Hour	Summary of Events and Information	Remarks and references to Appendices
OUTTERSTEENE	1.2.16	7 p.m.	17 cases admitted (no wounded); 18 evacuated or discharged to duty	
"	2.2.16	"	16 " " " " : 15 " " " " "	
"	3.2.16	"	19 " " " " : 19 " " " " "	
"	4.2.16	"	15 " " " " : 15 " " " " "	
"	5/6/2/16	"	109 " " " " : 109 " " " " "	
"	"	"	Received orders to have unit ready to move at nine hours notice.	
"	11/2/16	"	Schemes for concentration of Division if necessary are :— 1. Evacuation by 5 Corps area. 2. 5th Corps area. One section of 7.O. kept packed ready to move, other so that 5 units be ready on 3 hours notice.	
"	13/2/16	"	Message M385 from A. Gen. S. that normal conditions may be resumed.	
"	15/2/16	"	101 cases admitted (one wounded); 101 evacuated or discharged to duty. One wounded was from 13th Cheshires slight — due to aeroplane bomb.	
"	26/2/16	"	Received orders to hold unit in readiness to move on 9 hours notice.	
"	26/2/16	"	101 cases admitted (1 wounded officer); 101 evacuated or discharged to duty. (Bomb)	

H.W. Doggellen
Lt Col. M.C.
a.c. 76 W. F.A.

Army Form C. 2118.

WAR DIARY
or
INTELLIGENCE SUMMARY.
(Erase heading not required.)

MARCH 1916

Instructions regarding War Diaries and Intelligence Summaries are contained in F.S. Regs., Part II. and the Staff Manual respectively. Title pages will be prepared in manuscript.

Place	Date	Hour	Summary of Events and Information	Remarks and references to Appendices
OUTERSTEENE	5/3/16	7 p.m	Cases admitted for week ending 4th 100 (4 accidentally wounded). Cases evacuated 100 discharges to duty 100.	
"	8/3/16	"	Received orders from G.O.C. 74th Brigade that the section of the F.A. stationed at LA CRECHE would proceed on that farenoon of the 9th to Billets at farm HUILLEBET MAP 36A 7.19 15 7.8	11 FMD
"	9/ "	"	Received orders from A.D.M.S. to move 1st and 2nd lines & the 3rd F.A. from OUTTERSTEENE to join the remaining section at HUILLEBET	12 FMD
"	10/ "	"	Received orders to march from HUILLEBET MAP 36A 7.19.B.7.8. to Billets at MAP 36A squares 28 + 34, starting point 29.B.10.4 at 10 am.	13 FMD
"	10/ "	"	Reached Billets near Railway Station. HAM-EN-ARTOIS at 2.30 pm.	
"	11/ "	"	Received orders to march from Billets at HAM EN ARTOIS to Billets at BAILLEUL-AUX-CORNAILLES, starting point- Road Junction East of J.8 in LIETTES ref. map HAZEBROUCK 5a + LENS 11. 90 cases admitted during the week + 90 discharged to duty or evacuated	14 FMD
"	12/ "	7.30	Marched according to orders + reached Billets about 7 p.m. The road was about 21½ miles + the roads very heavy in places and men felt cut. On heavy roads two horses are not enough for a loaded Ambulance waggon, 4 mules would be much more suitable for these waggons than two horses.	15 FMD
"	18/ "	7pm	75 Cases admitted to hospital 56 cases evacuated or discharged to duty. Position of present of 7.F.A. Ref. map LENS 11. 7.2, north of Chocques. BAILLEUL-AUX-CORNAILLES.	16 FMD
"	25/ "	"	90 Cases admitted to hospital; 69 Cases evacuated or discharged duty; 29 Remained.	17 FMD

H.W. Davidson
Lt. Col. R.A.M.C.
O.C. 3 F.A.

WAR DIARY or INTELLIGENCE SUMMARY

Army Form C. 2118. Vol 8

75th F.A.

Place	Date	Hour	Summary of Events and Information	Remarks and references to Appendices
ECOIVRES	30/6		Routine. Evacuation of cases from the Right sector of the line held by the 25th Div. The main dressing station of the 75th F.A. is at ECOIVRES (map ref F.13.a.6.2.) situated in a school capable of accommodating about 30 cases, in addition there is a large marquee with good facilities for loading cases in case of a rush, a large mess room and be well with. There are two advanced dressing stations one at AUX-RIETZ (31.13.A.8.2.6.6.) & one at NEUVILLE-St-VAAST (31.3.A.8.C.6.2). The AUX-RIETZ station is used for walking cases for loading on to the Motor Ambulance Cars. The cases from NEUVILLE-ST-VAAST are brought down on wheeled stretchers to AUX-RIETZ at night. All the evacuation from the front line is done at night, along the AUX-RIETZ — The BRUNEHAUT-ARRAS - ECOIVRES road. The dug outs at the NO.3 are well protected by tunnelled deep dug outs is being constructed. The doors of the dug outs are protected by curtains belonging to the ambulance, have been placed in position. One section of the Ambulance is stationed at the No.3 & two lorries at the main dressing station. One half section is changed over every week.	

W.D. Waugher
Lt.Col. RAMC
O.C. 75th F.A.

25th 19—

No. 75 F. Amb.

COMMITTEE FOR THE
MEDICAL HISTORY OF THE WAR
Date 9 – JUN. 1915

Army Form C. 2118.

WAR DIARY
or
75th F.A. INTELLIGENCE SUMMARY. APRIL 1916

Instructions regarding War Diaries and Intelligence Summaries are contained in F.S. Regs., Part II. and the Staff Manual respectively. Title pages will be prepared in manuscript.

(Erase heading not required.)

Place	Date	Hour	Summary of Events and Information	Remarks and references to Appendices
BAILLEUL CORNVILLE	1/4/16	7 p.m.	107 admissions to hospital for week ending op.31st; 77 Evacuated to discharged tedy; 41 remaining.	M.49
"	8/4/16	"	104 " " " op.8 " 75 - " "	1.4.40
"	15/4/16	"	93 " " " op.15th; 46 " "	1.4.40
"	16/4/16	"	Received orders to take over positions in this line as occupied by 46th Div. on 20th	4.4.40
"	17/4/16	"	Sent 1 Officer, 3 O.R. as advance party & personally inspected junctions of roads & A.D. stations, main dressing stations &c.	18.4.40
"	19/4/16	"	1 M.E.O. + 14 men sent to CAPRO as our A.D.S., + transport to H.Q. Officers rest on 17th.	1.4.40
ECOIVRES	20/4/16		Two sections moved at 8 A.M. from BAILLEUL-AUX-CORNEILLES & arrived at ECOIVRES via F/3A. V.32 at 12.30 p.m. Took over main dressing station & 60 patients & sent 1 Officer + 2 O.R.s as a party reinforcement to MDS with suitable equipment. Left at BAILLEUL to hand over Hospital + Billets. One section. List of Billets, Wards to relieving unit, with particulars & patients. Names of proprietors &c. Left in the PM the section to march to ECOIVRES at 8 am. on 21st. 68 Patients admitted or taken over in hours, discharged nil	M.40
"	21st	"	20 Officer 27 O.Rs admitted, 10 discharged to CCS or duty.	"
"	22nd	"	38 O.R.s admitted, 2 Officers (1 wounded); at 1 O.R. discharged this 79 remaining in hosp. (notes)	M.40
"	23rd	"	28 O.R.s discharged duty for evacuation CCS	M.40

Army Form C. 2118.

WAR DIARY
or
INTELLIGENCE SUMMARY. 75th F.A.

(Erase heading not required.)

Instructions regarding War Diaries and Intelligence Summaries are contained in F. S. Regs., Part II. and the Staff Manual respectively. Title pages will be prepared in manuscript.

Place	Date	Hour	Summary of Events and Information	Remarks and references to Appendices
ECOIVRES	24/4/16	7pm	Admissions to Hosp. 20 (1 wounds); 5 cases evacuated or discharged to duty.	1=20
"	25/4 "	"	" 98 (1 Officer 4 O.R.s); 26 " " "	1=90
"	26 "	"	" 25 (" 5 "); 40 " " "	1=20
			24 heavy + 2 motor Ambulance cars were ordered to be held in readiness to assist in the collection of wounded. The sick wounded in this sector are line held by the Division. The sick wounded in this sector are evacuated by the 77th F.A.	
"	27/4 "	"	admissions 36; (wounded 7); evacuated or discharges to duty 33.	1=36
"	28/4 "	"	" 14; (1 Officer 2 O.R.s); " " " 39.	1=43
"	29/4 "	"	" 23 (wounds 10); " " " 24	1=50
"	30 " "	"	" 13 (" 4); " " " 14	1=22

H.E. Davis Cobry
2t. Col. (RAMC)
O.C. 75th F.A.

□ Main dressing Station
○ Advanced dressing Station
▷ Reg. Aid posts.

→ TO LENS
LES TILLEULS
NEUVILLE - St VAAST
AUX RIETZ
77th F.A.
1/2 Highland F.A.
51st Div.
→ TO SOUCHEZ
Left sector 25th Div.
77th F.A.
LA TARGETTE
→ TO ARRAS
Fme BRUNEHAUT
MAROEUIL
MONT St ELOY
77 F.A.
ECOIVRES.
25th F.A.

No. 75. 4. Cont.

May 1916.

COMMITTEE FOR THE
MEDICAL HISTORY OF THE WAR

Date 26 JUN '16

WAR DIARY
or
INTELLIGENCE SUMMARY. 73rd F.A.

Army Form C. 2118.

Vol 9

(Erase heading not required.)

Place	Date	Hour	Summary of Events and Information	Remarks and references to Appendices
ECOINRES	1.5.16	7 pm	Admissions 25 (wounded 1) discharges & evacuations 15.	T.2.W
"	2.5.16	"	" 22 (" 4) " " 20.	" " "
"	3.6.16	"	" 37 (" 4) " " 16.	" " "
			All apparatus for kitchen as aerial gas attack is now in working order. Doors of dugouts are protected by rolled & weighted blankets & double entrance to each dugout. Stretchers having places before the dressing room. Gangs have been placed at available points as far as Cayeux & orders published as to what each man is to do in case of attack.	
"	4. "	"	" admissions 27 (wounded 10, 30 O.R) discharges & evacuations 31	man
"	5. "	"	" " 24 (" 1 " ") " " 23 (67 remaining)	man
"	6. "	"	" " 17 (" " ") " " 17	man
"	7. "	"	" " 12 (" 2 " ") " " 19 (37 remaining)	man
"	8. "	"	" " 17 (" 1 " ") " " 19	man
"	9. "	"	" " 29 (" 3 " ") " " 33	man
"	10. "	"	" " 13 (" 5 " ") " " 18	man
"	11. "	"	" " 27 (" 8 " ") " " 26 (35 remaining)	man
"	12. "	"	" " 18 (" 5 " ") " " 27 (20 ")	man
"	13. "	"	" " 18 (" 1 " ") " " 16 (22 ")	man
"	14. "	"	" " 11 (" 1 " ") " " 9 (24 ")	man

WAR DIARY
INTELLIGENCE SUMMARY. 75th F.A.

Army Form C. 2118.

Place	Date	Hour	Summary of Events and Information	Remarks and references to Appendices
ECOIVRES	15/4/16	7 p.m.	Admissions 31; wounded —; discharged or evacuated 11; Received 44	
"	16/5/16		Received operation order No. 8 an attack to be made on left sector of the line by 25th Div. min's the opening ordered to have lunches & cars ready to evacuate if called on.	
"	17/5/16		Admissions 35; wounded 14; discharged or evacuated 38; remaining ? 32. 8 Stretcher squads sent to help to evacuate cases from the left sector at 2.30 p.m.	
"	18/5/16		Admissions 24; wounded 5; discharged or evacuated 28; remaining 26. 4 Stretcher squads sent to assist in left sector.	
"	19/5/16		Received R.T.M.C. order No. 10 re move to new area. Selected an motor. Route to 13 AILETTE – AUX – CORNAILLES at 8.30 b. am 19/5/16. Admissions 11; wounded 2; evacuated discharged Stretcher - 10; Remaining 31	
			" 28 " " " 18 " " " 30 " " 24	
"	20/5/16		B Section marched out 8.30 a.m. for BAILEUL – AUX – CORNAILLES with Copthorn.	
"	21/5/16		Admissions 22; 6 wounded; evacuated discharged 7; remaining 38. 19 ; 2 " " 29 " "	
"	22/5/16		" 27 ; 12 " " " 22 The nurses ordered in R.T.M.C order No 11 to proceed 10 post-passes the section already moved to BAILLEUL to remain there.	

Army Form C. 2118.

WAR DIARY
or
INTELLIGENCE SUMMARY. 75th — 7. A.

(Erase heading not required.)

Place	Date	Hour	Summary of Events and Information	Remarks and references to Appendices
ECOIVRES	22.5.16	7 p.m.	On night of 21st/22nd Sherbourne Amb. Car No. 9881 while waiting at Aux-Rietz Collecting Station was struck by the explosion of a gas shell & the radiator, lamps & mudguards injured. This happens about 1.57.30am. The drivers were No. 054091 Pte E.J. DAVIS & No. 116625 Pte J. HATE, who escaped. The car was repaired again in an hour. Went up to P's edeh on the left & arranged a round for evacuating Cases from the Quarries to NEUVILLE-ST-VAAST in case the 77th F.A. required assistance to one of their ordinary routes of evacuation was closed.	
"	23rd	"	Admissions 69; wounded 40; Evacuated & discharged to duty 68. Many other wounded came from the sector occupied by the 7th Brigade (P's action)	
"	24th	"	Admissions 46; wounded 22; Evacuated & discharged to duty 42.	
"	25th	"	" 36; " 12; " 35.	
"	26th	"	" 22; " 8; " 26.	
"	27th	"	" 22; " 7; " 14; Remained 8.	
"	28th	"	" 40; " 19; " 32.	
"	29th	"	" 46; " 21; " 39; " 60.	
"	30th	"	" 25; " 5; " 41.	

Army Form C. 2118.

WAR DIARY
or
INTELLIGENCE SUMMARY. 75th to 7 A.

(Erase heading not required.)

Instructions regarding War Diaries and Intelligence Summaries are contained in F.S. Regs., Part II. and the Staff Manual respectively. Title pages will be prepared in manuscript.

Place	Date	Hour	Summary of Events and Information	Remarks and references to Appendices
ECOIVRES	30/8	7 p.m	Received R.A.M.C. order No 11, Relief of 25th Div. by 51st. 75th F.A. to be relieved by 1st/2 Highland F.A. A.D.S. partly to be relieved night of 31/8/15. Main dressing station & Wounded - over night of 31/8/1 & 75th F.A. Bivouack at 10 p.m. that night to finish & 1/2 at 75th F.A. Bivouack at 10 p.m. to 1/2st 1st Highland 1st Bn 13 AILLEUL - AUX - PT NAILLES	
"	31st	"	Handed over advanced dressing stations at AUX-MIETZ & NEUVELLE - ST-VAAST to 1/2 1st Highland F.A. & handed in lists for evacuation of O + R parties which were held by the 75th & 7th Brigades of the 25th Div. Admissions 6; wounded 1; evacuations to Dieppe 25; New cases 23	

H.R.Davidson
Lt. Col. R.A.M.C.
O.C. 75th Field Ambulance

23rd Div.

No 45 Field Ambulance

June 1916

Army Form C. 2118.

75 Fd Amb June

WAR DIARY
or
INTELLIGENCE SUMMARY.

(Erase heading not required.)

Instructions regarding War Diaries and Intelligence Summaries are contained in F. S. Regs., Part II. and the Staff Manual respectively. Title pages will be prepared in manuscript.

Place	Date	Hour	Summary of Events and Information	Remarks and references to Appendices
ECOIVRES	1/6	7 p.m.	Handed over the dressing station & billets occupied by this unit into 1/2 Highland F.A. 17 patients in hospital handed over all belonging to divisions other than 25th.	1440
BAILLEUL-AUX-CORNAILLES	2/6	"	Marches from ECOIVRES at 10 p.m. night of 1/2nd arrives at BAILLEUL-AUX-CORNAILLES at 3.15 a.m. on 2nd. No men fell out on march. Admissions 20, evacuations to public charge 15, 5 remaining in hospital.	1440
"	10/6	"	"	1440
"	13/6	"	" 79 : 60	1440
HERICOURT	14/6	"	Received orders to march at 8 a.m. 14th to HERICOURT. Ref Lens 11. C.a. Arrived at HERICOURT at 12.20 p.m. No men fell out on the march. Received orders to march from HERICOURT to NOEUX (Road, O.H.) passing thro' cross roads at LIGNY-SUR-CANCHE at 10.30 a.m.	1440
NOEUX	15/6	"	Marched off at 8 A.M. and arrived at NOEUX at 12.30 p.m. Successful evacuation route to the stationary hospital.	1440
"	16/6	"	TREVENT. One man fell out and was included.	1440
"	17/6	"	Received orders to march from NOEUX to EPECAMPS (Lens 11, B. 6.) to form the advance at ST ACHEUL at 11 p.m.	1440
EPECAMPS	18/6	"	Marched according to orders & arrived at EPECAMPS at 1.30 a.m. Received evacuation orders No 42 to march from EPECAMPS at 10.30 p.m. to ST PECEUL	1440

Army Form C. 2118.

WAR DIARY
or
INTELLIGENCE SUMMARY. War Diary 78th F.A
(Erase heading not required.)

Instructions regarding War Diaries and Intelligence
Summaries are contained in F. S. Regs. Part II.
and the Staff Manual respectively. Title pages
will be prepared in manuscript.

Place	Date	Hour	Summary of Events and Information	Remarks and references to Appendices
BERTEAUCOURT	24/6/16	7 pm	Arrived at BERTEAUCOURT (Lens 11, O.6.) at 1.30 a.m.	
"	25/6/16	"	Received R.A.M.C. order No 15 & 74th Inf. Bgde. M.O. No 10, awarded order Bn. O 549. march to BONNEVILLE (Lens 11, 6.D.) passing road junction north of "Tir LE SOUDET at 10.25 p.m.	
BONNEVILLE	25/6/16	"	Reached BONNEVILLE at 12.30 a.m. Marches according to orders in line parties & convoy at 2.30 p.m. to 3 p.m. the head - forty arrives in TALMAS (Lens 11, 6.D.)	
TALMAS	27/6/16	"	Received R.A.M.C. order No 17 to march to TOUTENCOURT (Lens 11, 7, 6.) Starting point TALMAS at 9.30 p.m.	
TOUTENCOURT	28/6/16	"	Reached TOUTENCOURT at 12.30 p.m., one man fell out on the March. Received R.A.M.C order No.18 to march to HARPONVILLE (Lens 11, Q.6.) Memo dated H.Q. 28/6/16 Cancelling R.A.M.C order No 18.	
"	30/6/16	11 am	Received R.A.M.C. order No 19, ordering move in R.A.M.C. order No 18 to be carried out on 30th JUNE.	
HARPONVILLE	"	7 pm	Arrived in HARPONVILLE (Lens 11, Q.6.) & bivouacked at 3 p.m.	
"	1/6	9.30 pm	Received 25th Div. order No 79 to march immediately to CONTAY (Lens 11, 7.6.). Arrived at 11 p.m. & occupied huts in a wood to the N.E. of VADENCOURT.	

T W Davidson
Lt. Col. R.A.M.C
O.C. 75th F.A.

25th Division

75 Field Ambulance

COMMITTEE FOR THE
MEDICAL HISTORY OF THE WAR
Date 31 AUG 1915

July 1916
51

WAR DIARY
or
INTELLIGENCE SUMMARY. 76th 7 7's 3 Army

Army Form C. 2118.

25 July
Vol 11

Place	Date	Hour	Summary of Events and Information	Remarks and references to Appendices
VADENCOURT / CONTAY	1/7	9.30pm	Received 25th Div. Order No 79 to move immediately from HAPPONVILLE (Lens 11, C.6) to CONTAY (Lens 11, 7.6). Arrived at 11 p.m. & occupied huts in a wood to the N.E. of CONTAY.	14td
"	2nd	12.30pm	Received orders to send 75th 7.F.A. & at disposal of 32nd Div. & take over ready formed when ordered, the 32nd Div. is in the line in front of THIEPVAL (Lens 11, I.6). (M.V. 582 A.D.M.S., 25th Div.)	
"	"	4 pm	Received notice that the above orders are cancelled. (Memo # D.M.S.25D) 14td	
"	3rd	11am	Received orders to be in readiness to relieve the 25th Div. taking over the line from the 32nd.	
"	"	7.25pm	Received memo enclosed from T.M.O. order No.20 A to march at 7.30 pm on 3rd to BOUZINCOURT (Lens 11, H.6) & take over from the 90th 7.F.A. Marched accordingly & arrived at 10 p.m. to open the dressing station & marched the Bearer Division & one Cart Sub. division to the A.D.S. at BLACKHORSE BRIDGE (W.G.a.22. Sheet 57D)	14ns
BOUZINCOURT	4th	7 pm	The Bearer division of 77th 7.A. under orders of O.C 75th 7.A marched to the A.D.S at AVELUY (W.11. d.6.4. Sheet 57D). The Bearer division of 76th 7.A. was also placed under the orders of O.C 76th 7.A.I distributed as follows, one Sub-div. at BLACKHORSE BRIDGE & one at AVELOY, the other Sub-div. at AVELOY & the tenth back to WAIPLOY. No of cases evacuated from 1 a.m to 12 midnight 4.7.16 Officers /4 O.R 293	14ns

2353 Wt. W2544/1454 700,000 5/15 D.D.&L. A.D.S.S./Forms/C. 2118.

Army Form C. 2118.

WAR DIARY
or
INTELLIGENCE SUMMARY. 75th 7.A.

(Erase heading not required.)

Place	Date	Hour	Summary of Events and Information	Remarks and references to Appendices
BOUZINCOURT	5.7.16	9 am	Number of patients passed through A.D.S BOUZINCOURT from midnight 4th to midnight 5th. Officers 13 - (3 sick) O.R. 162 - (20 ")	2
"	"	"	Received from A.D.M.S. M.V. No. 611 at 12 midnight to withdraw one bearer Sub-division from the A.D.S. BOUZINCOURT to join the 74th Brigade. There were two bearers & wounded last night belonging to the 76th 7.A. Lieut: Clarke R.A.M.C. + one Sub-div. were withdrawn from BLACKHORSE BRIDGE A.D.S. The remaining bearer Sub-div. of 76th 7.A. was withdrawn from AVELUY A.D.S. & sent to join 74th Brigade. 5 ambulance cars + two Ford cars sent to join 76th 7.A. bearers with 74th Brigade. THIEPVAL AVENUE Aid Post has been taken over by the 49th Division.	
"	7.7.16		Number passed through A.D.S from midnight 5th to midnight 6th. Officers 7 wounded, 1 Rickets. O.R. 207 walking cases 46 stretcher " 1 Gemans	1600
"	"		Memo from A.D.M.S. dated 7.7.16 7th 7.A. from here line. This bearer div. departed at 10.30 pm.	

WAR DIARY or INTELLIGENCE SUMMARY. 78th F.A.

Army Form C. 2118.

Place	Date	Hour	Summary of Events and Information	Remarks and references to Appendices
BOUZINCOURT	8/7/16		Received message M.V. 6276 7/7/16 ordering withdrawal of another Sub-division of 77th K.F.A. which orders for it to march to ACHEUX at 10 a.m. 8th July. Also the ready to hand over to incoming unit. Numbers passed through dressing station from midnight 6th to midnight 7th. Officers 13; O.R's 260's. Germans 9. There are sanitation 9th and Captured withdrew Risdent & dressing station at MILLENCOURT.	
MILLENCOURT	9/7/16		Sent an advance party to link away main dressing station at 9 a.m. from 36th F.A., 12th F.A. Div., & the 32nd Div. 37th F.A. were the Beaver Div. 76th F.A. who were attached to the 32nd Div. ordered to take over the Orders Post (leaving 16th Brig. 32nd Div. The Beaver Div. 77th F.A. part J which has been assisting 32nd Div. were ordered to take over a post on the BAPAUME ROAD behind the 74th Brigade, 25th Div. This Brigade were occupying enemy trenches from LA BOISSELLE to the BAPAUME ROAD. The Beaver Div. 76th F.A. was withdrawn from the post at BLACKHORSE BRIDGE near ATHUILE. The post being handed over to the 1st/3rd West-Riding F.A., 49th Div. The Beaver Div. & one (2nd Rub.) div 75th F.A. with 9 horse ambulance wagons + two limber waggons have been Carl-were ordered to take over the A.D.S. at NORTH CHIMNEY ALBERT, which was used as a main dressing station by 37th F.A., 12th Div.	

2353 Wt. W2541/1454 700,000 5/15 D. D. & L. A.D.S.S./Forms/C. 2118.

Army Form C. 2118.

WAR DIARY
or
INTELLIGENCE SUMMARY. 75th F.A.

(Erase heading not required.)

Instructions regarding War Diaries and Intelligence Summaries are contained in F. S. Regs., Part II. and the Staff Manual respectively. Title pages will be prepared in manuscript.

Place	Date	Hour	Summary of Events and Information	Remarks and references to Appendices
MILLENCOURT	9/16		Number of cases passed through main dressing station, MILLENCOURT from BOUZINCOURT from midnight 8th to midnight 9th:— 136 O.R's, 1 Officer.	
"	10/16		The dressing station at BOUZINCOURT was handed over to the 91st F.A. 32nd Div. at 8 a.m. on the 9th. The Beam Dressing 76th F.A. was partly relieved at MEDVILLERS but by 75th F.A., the bearers of 76th being placed at reserve. The remainder of the Beam dis. of 76th relieved & placed in reserve at MILLENCOURT. Received notice that OVILLERS + OVILLERS POST would be taken over by 32nd Div. A.D.M.S., so the 75th F.A. has been practically serving two Divisions, viz:— 14th Aug, 32nd Div. from OVILLERS + 75th Brig, 25th Div, from BAPAUME ROAD POST. Gave orders to withdraw bearers from OVILLERS (except a party to act as guides) as soon as the relieving bearers arrived. Cases passed this from midnight 9th & their night 10th: 131 O.R's Officers, 8. A.D.S. ALBERT 10 O.R's, 4 Officers.	

WAR DIARY

INTELLIGENCE SUMMARY. 75th W. F. A.

Army Form C. 2118.

Place	Date	Hour	Summary of Events and Information	Remarks and references to Appendices
MILLENCOURT	11/7/16		Cases admitted from mid night 10th to midnight 11th. Officers wounded 1. O.R's 95. Germans wounded 5. Sick 23. The 2/5th Div. Reg. Aid Posts are now in the B + P LIME ROAD; the motor and the A.D.S is on the B + P LIME ROAD; the motor Ambulance cars run up to the A.D.S. with Cars are taken from there to MILLENCOURT + evacuated from there by M.A.C cars to PUCHEVILLERS. So far there has not been much difficulty in evacuation + wheeled stretchers can be used. A good part of the way. One Bearer Division is kept at the A.D.S in dig outs near the regimental aid posts, one bearer division in support at North Ghissing Albert, and one in rest at MILLENCOURT. One tent sub division at North @HIMNEY ALBERT	Paras thro' A.D.S ALBERT. O.R's 12. Le BOISSELL village
"	12th		+ two at MILLENCOURT. Officers 1, O.R's 94. A.D.S ALBERT. O.R's 38. admitting 11th - 12th 77th F.A. Bearers at BAPAUME ROAD Post relieved by 75th F.A. Bearers Kus	

WAR DIARY
or
INTELLIGENCE SUMMARY. 75th F.A.

Army Form C. 2118.

Place	Date	Hour	Summary of Events and Information	Remarks and references to Appendices
MILLENCOURT	13/7/16		Admissions during 24 hours wounded Officers 5; O.R's 51; Germans 1. Sick O.R's 23.	
"	14/7/16		the Beaver 75th F.A. wounded. " " " wounded Officers 4; O.R's 67. " " " Sick " 2; " 18. One Bearer 75th F.A. killed. The regimental aid posts were advanced, one beyond the village of La BOISSELL. Ambulance Cars & cars were now within 100 yds. of their village if necessary.	
"	15/7/16		Bearer Division 75th F.A. relieved by Bearer division 76th F.A. under Lieut. Clarke R.M.C. Admissions wounded Officers 8; O.R's 176. (incl.) wounded shellshock from DRILLERS. " " " Sick " ; " 16. A large proportion of these cases were stretcher cases as many of the lightly wounded walk down to ALBERT have been & come to MILLENCOURT.	
"	16/7/16		Admissions Officers wounded 6; O.R's 101. " Sick 1; " 24.	

WAR DIARY
or
INTELLIGENCE SUMMARY. 75th F.A.

Army Form C. 2118.

Place	Date	Hour	Summary of Events and Information	Remarks and references to Appendices
MILLENCOURT	17/7/16		Admissions Officers wounded 3-; O.R's 27. Sick 9. Most of this came was from the attack on officers, the 12th Division left the line on the early morning of 17th and only line or white cases of wounds were admitted up to 6 a.m. The 48th Division took over the evening before at MILLENCOURT & ALBERT (NORTH CHIMNEY) & Collecting Post on the BAPAUME ROAD from the 75th & 77th F.A. on the afternoon of the 17th according to A.D.M.S. order No. 24. The Premier divisions of the 76th & 77th F.A.'s with their transport rejoined their units & the 75th F.A. marched to Millencourt. Received R.T.M.O. order No 2.5 to march to Millencourt - BEAUVAL.	
SENLIS	18"			
BEAUVAL	19"		Arrived at this place about 5 p.m. on 18th. Started to refit - the men took hot baths - transport and equipment - a certain amount of equipment was destroyed by Rifle fire at PLAT KITHORSE BRIDGE by A.S.S.S. equipment - mess tins and Lost Col. the A.D.S. had	

WAR DIARY or INTELLIGENCE SUMMARY

Army Form C. 2118.

75th F.A.

Place	Date	Hour	Summary of Events and Information	Remarks and references to Appendices
Bus-les-ARTOIS	20th July		Received R.A.M.C. order No. 26, to relieve Ambulances of 12th Div.	
"	21st		Marched to Bus-les-ARTOIS in 2 F.A.	
"	22nd		Reached Bus at 4.30 p.m. & took over from 37th F.A.	
"	23rd		Received R.A.M.C. order No. 27, to relieve Ambulances of 29th Div. at SARTON, Div. rest Station.	
"	23rd		Sent one section under Captain R. of R.A.M.C. and one sub section.	
SARTON	24th		Marched at 9 a.m. + arrived at SARTON 11.30 a.m. + took over hospital + billets from Ambulance of 29th Div. Found 120 patients in hospital, 67 of these were discharged. Stuff of the O.C.S. there was also a large quantity of blankets, stretchers, dressings etc., much of this material was useless & had to be returned. All the unnecessary articles are to be sent back to reserve in Salvage empty billets had to be policed & sheets spread out. Received R.A.M.C. order No. 28, to take over from 3rd Field Ambulance 29th Div.	
"	27th		VAUCHELLES av D.R.S.	
VAUCHELLES	28th		Marched at 10 a.m. & took over from 3rd Ft. Field Ambulance at VAUCHELLES.	

WAR DIARY
or
INTELLIGENCE SUMMARY. 75 & 7 A.
(Erase heading not required.)

Army Form C. 2118.

Place	Date	Hour	Summary of Events and Information	Remarks and references to Appendices
RUCHELLES	31.7.16	7pm	Collected all equipment from 3 A.T.P.W. & right bank & left bank, which was put in charge of one N.C.O. & one nurse. Blanket down folds & hospital clothing disinfected & washed & an inventory taken of all equipment & stores in use by mobilization. These extra stores are at V.Wd. # 5 & 6 S.? Patients admitted from 18th July after leaving the line. Officers 6; O.R.s 454. Evacuated officers 3; O.R.s 191. To duty " 1; O.R.s 180.	

H. E. Davidson
Lt Col. R.A.M.C.
O.C. 75th F.A.

Volume X   July 1916

Medical Services

75th Field Ambulance

R.A.M.C.

25th Nov.

75th Field Ambulance.

August 1916

COMMITTEE FOR THE
MEDICAL HISTORY OF THE WAR
Date −9 OCT. 1916

WAR DIARY
or
INTELLIGENCE SUMMARY. 75th F.A.

Army Form C. 2118.

Place	Date	Hour	Summary of Events and Information	Remarks and references to Appendices
LEALVILLERS	16th to 16		Reached destination at 2.45 p.m. + reoccupied billets.	
"	17/8/16		75th F.A. will relieve 1st West Riding F.A. West Riding F.A. will leave 2 Sections of 3 Officers + 20 O.R's to the rest, at 7 a.m. 18th Aug. R.A.M.C. orders 35 — to relieve 1st W. Riding F.A. in front area — to meet 15th — relief to be completed by 8 a.m. Transport to be back at HEDAUVILLE (P, 3, S, c.11.) 14. Gns 75th F.A. at W10, c.9.3. 75th F.A. to collect from rehab Divisional area, casualties by One Bearer Sub-div. of 77th F.A.	
Map 57 D. W.10.c.9.3.	18/8/16		A.D.S.'s AVELOY, BLACKHORSE BRIDGE + LANCASTER DUMP, collecting posts SWALLOW S N£92, + PAISLEY AVENUE. Relieves 1st West Riding F.A., relief completed by 7.30 a.m. Marches from HEDAUVILLE at 4 a.m.	
"	21		Relieves working party of 3rd W. Riding F.A. at new aid post Soudy Avenue by 40 men of 76th F.A. under Lieut. CLARKE R.A.M.C.	was

WAR DIARY

INTELLIGENCE SUMMARY. 75th F.A.

Army Form C. 2118.

Place	Date	Hour	Summary of Events and Information	Remarks and references to Appendices
W.10.c.9.3	21st		Two men of 75th F.A. killed to-day by shell fire while evacuating wounded, but other two men of squad escaped, they got the wounded under shelter + afterwards brought them down to the A.D.S. at No 4 post. An att[emp]t was made by the 7th Brigade 28th Div. on some trenches near the Leipzic Redoubt in conjunction with the 48th Div. on this night + after fight. The casualties were not heavy + many wounded (previous were found this) the A.D.S.'s including two officers.	
"	24th		The 7th Brigade attacked both the Hindenburg trench 25.8 Casus were evacuated from this Brigade alone mainly thro' BLACKHORSE A.D.S. besides about 30 enemy wounded. No difficulty was found in getting the cases away owing to the good work by all concerned, Officers, N.C.O's + men showing great initiative & courage under such conditions.	
"	25th		Counter Attacks + heavy shell fire. 176 Casus came thro' BLACKHORSE + 80 thro' PAISLEY Avenue, two bearers of 75th F.A. attached to 75th were killed three wounded, one bearer of (here)	

75th F.A.

WAR DIARY
INTELLIGENCE SUMMARY. 75th F.A.

Army Form C. 2118.

Place	Date	Hour	Summary of Events and Information	Remarks and references to Appendices
W10.C.9.3	26		Received R.A.M.C. order No. 3115 hand over the left section of the line between THIEPVAL Avenue relief to be completed by 8 a.m. on the 27th.	
	27		The cases were evacuated from BLACKHORSE A.D.S. 32 " " No 4 Post. 30 " " AVELUY. Handed over left section according to orders. Reserve places as follows: 3 Officers 1 oct. Sub. dist. 4 bearer div. 75th F.A. at BLACKHORSE BRIDGE. R.29 One N.C.O. + 23 men 77th (B) F.A. (attached) at AVELUY Took over Main dressing Station at VARENNES from 2nd West Riding F.A. Personnel 4 M.O.'s, 1 R.A. Mes. + 40 lent Sub-divisions.	
	28th		On the 27th the Casualties were 112 from BLACKHORSE 30 from AVELUY A.D.S. A report was received that there were always wounded in the trenches but this was not the case, as all	

WAR DIARY
or
INTELLIGENCE SUMMARY.

Army Form C. 2118.

(Erase heading not required.)

Place	Date	Hour	Summary of Events and Information	Remarks and references to Appendices
W.10.C.93	28		The Regtl. Aid Posts had easily been located 9 M.O.'s of Batt.'s in the line reported all doing even when Regtl. Aid Qrs. said there were wounded not removed. A map of reference was given & this was found to be one the Regtl. Aid Posts which was at Victoria Glen. If wounded squads waiting.	
"	29th		have been broken by shellfire. The banks of the river A NCRE above BLACKHORSE Br. Road the road to the A.D.S is now flooded.	
"	30		The road to the A.D.S near the marsh at BLACKHORSE is now impassable for cars, so a horse ambulance was employed to take the men down to the main road, in the dark the ambulance slipped off the narrow road, its deep mud & in attempts to extricate it, it was sometimes upset & broken & could not be got out. Horses were nearly drowned, but were rescued in time. The A VELOY A.D.S is now being used. The Cam being taken down there by wheel stretcher. This will be very difficult however if there is any heavy shelling.	
"	31st		Regtl Quiet. On 28 " 29th Div. front only 6 unfortunate few caus being James Strength	1st 8 days Jany Lts. Col. R. Bruce (?) O.C. 75 in ft (passed)

2353 Wt. W2544/1454 700,000 5/15 D. D. & L. A.D.S.S./Forms/C. 2118

Confidential

War Diary (Medical)

75th Field Ambulance

September 1916

Volume XII

WAR DIARY or INTELLIGENCE SUMMARY

Army Form C. 2118.

75" M" F.A.

Place	Date	Hour	Summary of Events and Information	Remarks and references to Appendices
VARENNES	1/10		Number of sick & wounded passed thro' the Advanced Dressing Station from the night of 18th/19th Aug. to 31st August. 15.35- headges a number of Lower wounded about 15 or 60. Number of sketcher cases passed thro' M.D.S. at Varennes from noon 28th to 31st Aug. Inclusive. Wounds 15-4, sick 18, lowered wounded 13.	11-a
"	2nd		Received read orders that the 7th & 75th Inf. Brigades would make an attack on the night of the 4th/5th Div. tomorrow on the hinders to the north of the LEIPSIC SALIENT towards THIEPVAL. Made all arrangements about evacuation from the line. The cases are dressed at the A.D.S. at BLACKHORSE BRIDGE & then passed down the A.D.S. at AVELOY where they are loaded on the Motor Ambulance & House Ambulance Cars, the walking cases go on to the Car Stand on the Pioneer road & are then run to CLAIREFAYE Farm on motor lorries. The sketcher cases are taken to the M.D.S at VARENNES.	
"	3rd		The attack was begun about 5.10 a.m. & by 8 a.m. about 70 walking cases and 8 sketcher cases had passed through the A.D.S.	11-a

Army Form C. 2118.

WAR DIARY
or
INTELLIGENCE SUMMARY. 75th F.A.

(Erase heading not required.)

Instructions regarding War Diaries and Intelligence Summaries are contained in F.S. Regs., Part II and the Staff Manual respectively. Title pages will be prepared in manuscript.

Place	Date	Hour	Summary of Events and Information	Remarks and references to Appendices
VARENNES	4.5.9.16		200 cases went thro' this Advanced dressing station up to about 6 p.m. All the Regt. Aid Posts were cleared & some cases known to be lying out beyond the front line could not be got till dark. About 30 more cases were got down at night from the front line beyond no man's land, the foremost being on [?] carrying the wounded I walking & stretcher cases (156 + 64) probably all the wounded were recovered.	(w)
	5h "		Received R.A.M.C. order no 39 that this Division should be relieved by this unit the M.D.S. at VATTENNES should be handed over to 35th F.A. by 12 noon on the 7th. O.C. 35th F.A. to send Advance party to the A.D.S. as equal number were withdrawn.	[?]
"	7h "		Handed over according to orders at 12 noon & marched to PUCHEVILLERS at 12.30 p.m.	
PUCHEVILLERS	9th "		Received 25th Div. order no. 123. 75th F.A. to march to BEAUVAL with 74th Brigade on the 10th.	
BEAUVAL	10th "		Rec. B.O.O. No 72 to march to St HILAIRE on the 11th.	
ST. HILAIRE	11th "		Rec. B.O.O. No 73 to march to REDERIE Ferme on the 12th.	was

WAR DIARY
or
INTELLIGENCE SUMMARY.
(Erase heading not required.)

Army Form C. 2118.

Place	Date	Hour	Summary of Events and Information	Remarks and references to Appendices
PEDERIE FARM	12/9/16		Reached PEDERIE Farm took up billets. Accommodation very poor, put-up canvas for the sick. Approach road very bad, first-aid trucks over the fields.	
"	15/9/16		Checked + refilled Unit-panniers + Medical equipment; with the exception of a few articles that the Advance Med. Stores has not in stock.	
"	24/9/16		Received B.O.O. No 75 that the Brigade would march to BEAUVAL on 25/9.	
"	25/9/16		Marched at 7.30 a.m. reached BEAUVAL 1.40 p.m. delayed one hour at starting point by traffic.	
BEAUVAL	26/9/16		Received R.A.M.C order No 42 to take over Officers Hospital + Rest Station at LOUVENCOURT by 12 noon 26". Issued 4 ORs to bit. stand on 26" at 10 p.m. + 30 O.R's to 96 & 98th F.A. Marched at 8 A.M. arrived at 11.55. advance party left at 5.30 a.m. Took over Hospital 14 Officers + 117 O.R's.	
LOUVENCOURT	30/9/16		Received R.A.M.C order No 44 to take over M.D.S. CLAIRFAYE FARM from 33rd F.A. on the 1/10/16.	

H.A. Davidson
Lt: Col R.A.M.C
O.O 75th F.A.

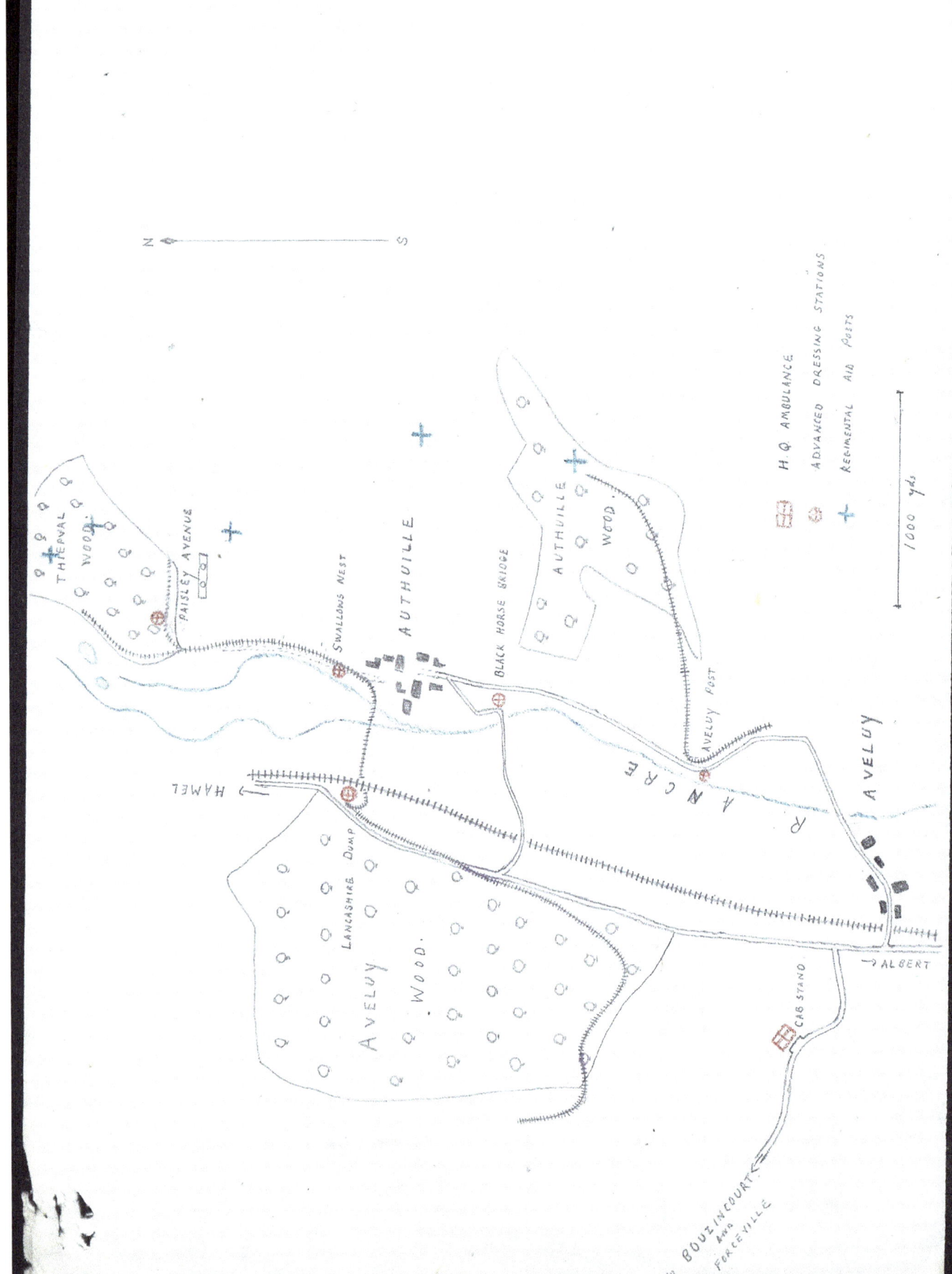

WAR DIARY or INTELLIGENCE SUMMARY

Army Form C. 2118.

75th F.A.

Place	Date	Hour	Summary of Events and Information	Remarks and references to Appendices
CLAIRFAYE	1/10/16		Took over dressing station at 12 noon. No O.R.'s to 12 midnight. 3 Officers 112 O.R.'s. Lieut. GREGORY ordered to report to A.D.M.S. detaining two officers fit for duty besides O.C. Received orders to pack up stores at LOUVENCOURT redistribution ready for a move, also to prepare stores over in D.g. CLAIRFAYE. Inventories of stores made out ready for handing over.	
"	2/10/16		Received R.A.M.C. order No 45. 75th F.A. orders the accommodation behind Civil Hospital at WARLOY over to EAST CLAIRFAYE to be handed over to V Corps at noon 2nd. Advance party from 6th F.A., V Corps arrived on the 1st 1 Officer & 10 O.R.'s. Received R.A.M.C. order No. 46 that EAST CLAIRFAYE would be handed over to 39th Div. F.A. 2nd Corps that 75th F.A. would take over accommodation near Civil Hosp. WARLOY on receipt of this order & to supply a party of 26 O.R.'s to Special Operating Centre WARLOY. marched with advance party & transport of one Section at 4.30 p.m.	

WAR DIARY or INTELLIGENCE SUMMARY.   75th F.A.

Army Form C. 2118.

Place	Date	Hour	Summary of Events and Information	Remarks and references to Appendices
WARLOY	2/10/16		Reached this Station at 6 pm. Detailed party from work in Special Hospital. Left 1 Officer & 4 O.R's at dressing station CLAIRFAYE & hand over.	
"	3/10/16		Advance party from F.A. 39th Div arrived Stationers CLAIRFAYE, all stores (cots), blankets & stationers handed over according ly. Death with at CLAIRFAYE from 1st – 2nd/10 160. No of cases dealt with at CLAIRFAYE from 1st – 2nd/10 160. " " " " 2nd Corps Rest Station LOUVENCOURT " " " from 2/9/16 to 5/10, 615.	
"	4/10/16 14/16		Number of cases dealt with at D.R.S WARLOY 2/10 to 14/10 400, (219 evacuated to C.C.S or discharged to duty). A new D.R.S (wooden huts) is being constructed by the Ambulance at SENLIS.	
"	6/10/16 18/10/16		Received R.A.M.C order No 58 that 75th F.A. will be in reserve as follows Zrd Division WARLOY, Bergen Div. AVELOY CHATEAU, Cors at BOUZINCOURT at zero hour.	

WAR DIARY
or
INTELLIGENCE SUMMARY. 76th F.A.

Army Form C. 2118.

Place	Date	Hour	Summary of Events and Information	Remarks and references to Appendices
WARLOY	19/10/16		Received A.D.M.S order S.B. 425 of 19.9.16 to let operations are postponed 24 hrs.	
"	21/10/16		Bearer division sent to AVELOY Chateau in reserve, (but div. in reserve at WATLOY. Bearers sent to assist 77th & 76th F.A. at POZIERES & DANUBE TRENCH, M.B.S. respectively.	
"	23rd		R.H. MC Order No. 51 ordering D.R.S. at WATLOY to be handed over to 32nd Div. Marched to VADENCOURT according to B.O.O. No 85.	
VADENCOURT	24th		Marched to BEAUVAL according to B.O.O. No 86	
BEAUVAL	29th		Received B.O.O No 87 to entrain at CANDAS on the 30th at 12.51 p.m.	
"	30th		Entrained & arrived at CAISITE about 9.20 p.m. detrained & marched to billets at FOURDOHILLE.	
FOURDOHILLE	31st		Received 7th B.O.O. to march to NIEPPE on the 1st Nov. B.O.M.C order No. 54. to relieve 21st F.A. with main dressing station at NIEPPE 13.16.c.6. A.D.S at W.19.d.1.5. PLOEGSTEERT.	

H.A Davidson
Lt Col. / Bm C
76th F.A.

25th Dec.

Nov 1916

14/8/2

1/5th Field Ambulance

COMMITTEE FOR THE
MEDICAL HISTORY OF THE WAR
Date -3 JAN. 1917

WAR DIARY
or
INTELLIGENCE SUMMARY.

Army Form C. 2118.

7.5.15 — 7.7.15

Place	Date	Hour	Summary of Events and Information	Remarks and references to Appendices
NIEPPE	1/5		Arrived according to orders & took over this M.D.S. at 7h.p.m. from 2 E A F. Takes the post of ROMARIN for the collection of sick. Bearers were placed in all the regimental aid posts. Officers in charge M.D.S. Captain A H HUYOFF & Lieut. BENT. Took over charge of M.D.S. at NIEPPE.	
"	2 "			
"	4 "		For week ending 4th — 139 cases admitted, 83 evacuated & discharged to duty. (11 O.R.s wounded).	
"	11 "		11 " 240 Cases admitted, 181 " (19 O.R.s wounded)	
"	18 "		18 " 180 cases admitted, 186 evacuated or discharged to duty, 48 remained. (24 O.R.s wounded)	
"	25 "		25 " 211 cases admitted, 203 evacuated on discharged to duty (10; 22 O.R.s wounded)	

NA Dendray
Lieut Col R.A.M.C.

26th Div.

140/900

45th Field Ambulance

Dec 1916

COMMITTEE FOR THE
MEDICAL HISTORY OF THE WAR
Date 31 JAN. 1917

Army Form C. 2118.

75. Field Ambulance

Vol / 6

WAR DIARY
or
INTELLIGENCE SUMMARY.
(Erase heading not required.)

Place	Date	Hour	Summary of Events and Information	Remarks and references to Appendices
NIEPPE	2/12/16	7 p.m.	Cases admitted for week ending 2/12/16 160 (Wounded 1(0), 21(O.R)). 168 evacuated or discharged to duty. 1.O., 36 O.R's remained.	
"	5th		Dressing post at ROMARIN handed over to 36th Div. Aid Post's at HYDE PARK CORNER taken over by 26th 75th F.A. remained. Aid Post's now being evacuated by the Bns + duties of Aid Post's now being evacuated by the Bns + duties of Dead Horse Corner, R.1365 House 56 + Wintage Hall. (Cases admitted for week ending 9/12/16 147 (wounded 20(ARs)). 147 evacuated or discharged to duty 25 remained.	
"	9th			
"	16th		Cases admitted for week ending 16/12/16 15-6 (3 O, 12 O.R's) 148 evacuated or discharged to duty. 1 Off, 29 O.R's remained. Building Details re at hand post, laying Gravier at A.D.S. sandbags renewed at dugouts, duck boards relayed drainage improved, dressing rooms white washed, painted + stove put in.	

2353 Wt. W25H/1454 700,000 5/15 D. D. & L. A.D.S.S./Forms/C. 2118.

Army Form C. 2118.

WAR DIARY
or
INTELLIGENCE SUMMARY.
(Erase heading not required.)

Instructions regarding War Diaries and Intelligence Summaries are contained in F. S. Regs., Part II. and the Staff Manual respectively. Title pages will be prepared in manuscript.

Place	Date	Hour	Summary of Events and Information	Remarks and references to Appendices
DIEPPE	23rd Dec.		Patients admitted for week ending 23rd: 132. (wounded 1 Officer, 9-O.Rs) Evacuated on discharge to duty: 132, remaining 32	14440
"	30 "		Patients admitted for week ending 30th: 178. (wounded 5 Officers 36 O.R.) Evacuated on discharge to duty: 191, remaining 23	14440

31/12/16

H.C. Davidson
Lt.Col. R.A.M.C.
O.C. 5th F.A.

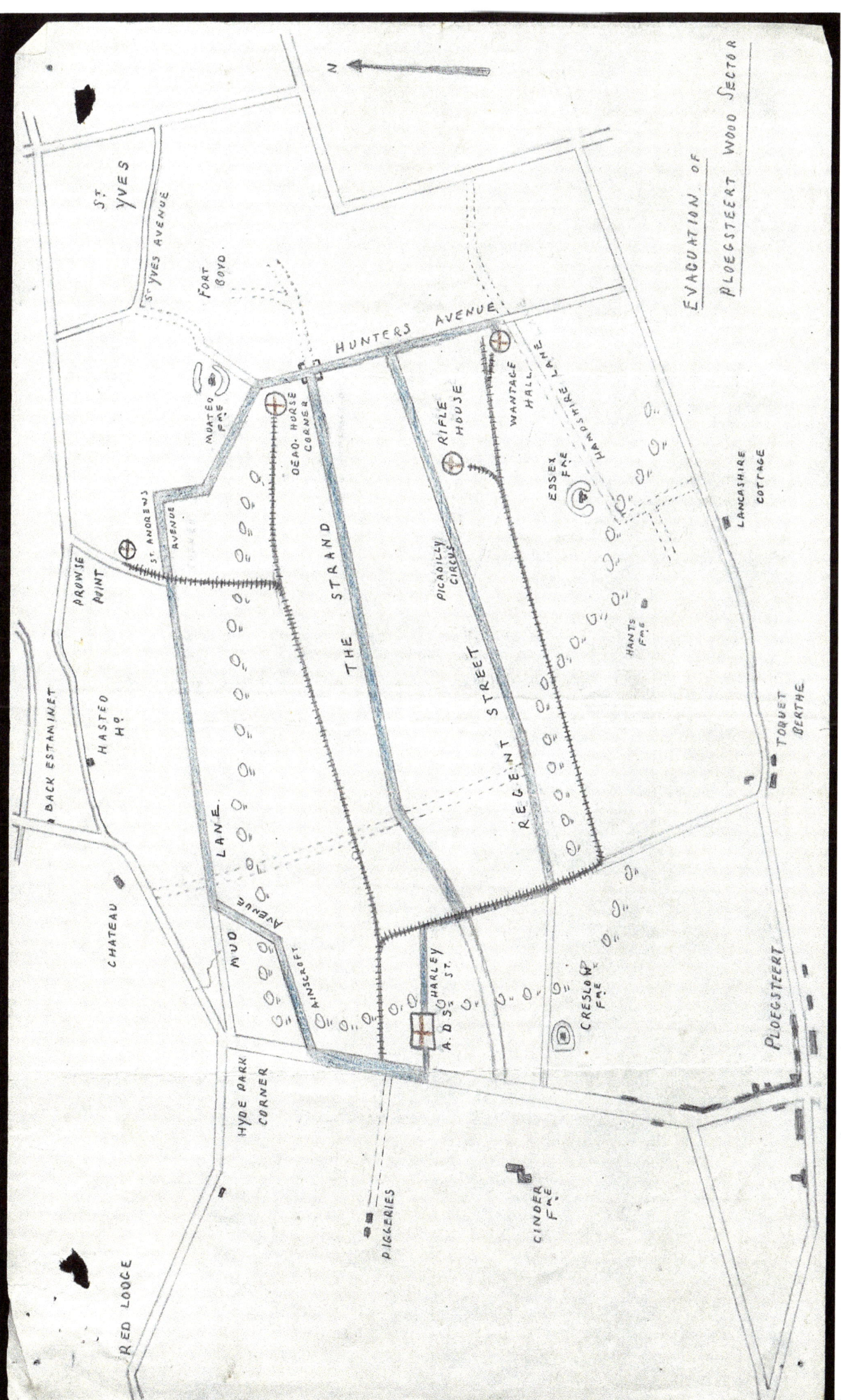

140/19-3

25th Div.

45th Field Ambulance

COMMITTEE FOR THE
MEDICAL HISTORY OF THE WAR
Date 13 MAR. 1917

WAR DIARY
or
INTELLIGENCE SUMMARY.   75th. Fld. Amb.
(Erase heading not required.)

Army Form C. 2118.

Vol 17

Instructions regarding War Diaries and Intelligence Summaries are contained in F. S. Regs., Part II. and the Staff Manual respectively. Title pages will be prepared in manuscript.

Place	Date	Hour	Summary of Events and Information	Remarks and references to Appendices
NIEPPE 7.4.17	7/7/17		Patients admitted for week ending 6/7/17 – 134. (wounded 14 ORs) " evacuated or discharged to duty 153, remaining 31.	
"	14/7 14th		" admitted for week ending 13/7/17 – 185 (wounded 145. 10 O.Rs). " evacuated or discharged to duty – 142, Remaining 74.	
"	21st		" admitted for week ending 20/7/7 – 179 (wounded 21 O.Rs) " evacuated or discharged to duty – 180 (Remains 72.)	
NIEPPE	28th		" admitted for week ending 27/7/17 – 241 (wounded 69, p. 30 ORs) " evacuated or discharged to duty – 213. The wounded were due to an attack by the 74th. Brigade from the arranged and lit for the collection & evacuation of the wounded works built, no signal difficulty was experienced. The assault opened on the 22nd of July. heavy shelling + all the wounded had reached the M.D.S shortly after 12 midnight.	

M.C. Davidson
25. C.A.M.C.

2353 Wt. W25141/1454 700,000 5/15 D. D. & L. A.D.S.S./Form/C. 2118.

COMMITTEE FOR THE
MEDICAL HISTORY OF THE WAR
Date 4 APR 1917

75 Field Ambulance

Army Form C. 2118.

WAR DIARY
or
INTELLIGENCE SUMMARY.
(Erase heading not required.)

95/18

Place	Date	Hour	Summary of Events and Information	Remarks and references to Appendices
NIEPPE	3/9/17		Patients admitted for week ending 3/9. 206 (wounded Offrs. 3; ORs. 27). Evacuated to Railways & Inf'y. 186.	
"	10/9/17		admitted for week ending 10/9. 179 (wounded Offrs. 11 OKs. 11). evacuated & discharged duty 175. (Running S.S.). L/Cpl. JAMES accidentally wounded by a bomb. 7.15 P.M. Pte. TILLING killed by shell fire at A.D.S. 7.15 P.M. N.E.	
"	17/9/17		Patients admitted for week ending 17/9. 190 (wounded Offrs. 5 ORs 109). Evacuated & discharged duty 248.	
"	20/9/17		Raid by 4th Aus. Bde. 19/9/17. 26 gas walking were Offr. 4. ORs. 92. Inmates of 28 mile lying cases. Medical arrangements satisfactory & carried out well with 2nd Army Extensions. Lorr'd train arrived without rest. 11.30am. and pts. were gradually cleared. At 2pm. Artillery bombardment of road began at 10.40 am. Unit relieved by 3rd N. Zealand F. Amb. Relief emptied at 7.30 am. and moved off to BAESTRE at 9am. Attached to 74th Inf. Bde.	My Ref HAZEBROUCK SA

Army Form C. 2118.

WAR DIARY
or
INTELLIGENCE SUMMARY.
(Erase heading not required.)

Instructions regarding War Diaries and Intelligence Summaries are contained in F. S. Regs., Part II. and the Staff Manual respectively. Title pages will be prepared in manuscript.

Place	Date	Hour	Summary of Events and Information	Remarks and references to Appendices
CAESTRE	21st		Moved off at 9.15 am to EBBLINGHEM	HAZEBROUCK y.A.
EBBLINGHEM	22nd		Moved off at 7.45 am to LEULINGHEM.	do.
LEULINGHEM	24th		Patients admitted for week ending 24/7/17. 175. (Wounded Offrs 1, O.Rs. 17.) evacuated to Hospital Ambulances 165. Transferred to 3" N.ZEALAND F.A. 54 (20 Sit). Unit in training. Great company interests shewn marching, thysical exercise, Inspections of equipment, men clothing, kits and general transport.	

J.F. Brown
Captain
for O/C 7 F.A.

2353 Wt. W2514/1454 700,000 5/15 D. D. & L. A.D.S.S./Forms/C. 2118.

Mar. 1917

25th Div.

75th Field Ambulance

140/2042

COMMITTEE FOR THE
MEDICAL HISTORY OF THE WAR
Date 11 MAY 1917

Army Form C. 2118.

WAR DIARY
or
INTELLIGENCE SUMMARY.
(Erase heading not required.)

75th F.A.

Place	Date	Hour	Summary of Events and Information	Remarks and references to Appendices
LEULINGHEM	3/3/17		Cases admitted for week ending March 3rd. O.Rs 3; Officers 3.	1 LED
"	10/3/17		Remarks - Discharges to duty 10	
"	11/3/17		Cases admitted for week ending March 10th: 72	1 RCID
			" discharges to duty 34.	
			Received orders to move to TATTINGHEM 9 a.m.	
TATTINGHEM	17/3/17		Arrived TATTINGHEM 10 A.M.	
"	17/3/17		Cases admitted 96, Discharges to duty 14, to Roll + H St. Hosp. 65. No 7 Con. Hosp. 21.	1 HAD
RENESCURE	20/3 "		Brigade order no 114, unit to move with Brigade this a.m. at - RENESCURE, marched 9 a.m., arrived 2 p.m.	
STRAZEELE	21/3 "		Brigade order no 115, Unit marched with Brigade to STRAZEELE marched 8:30 a.m. arrived 1 p.m.	
"	22/3 "		B.O, no 116 - Unit to march to billets at - A.18.d.6.2. map 36	
A.18.d.6.2	23/3 "		Arrived at 2:30 p.m. to take over huts & billets.	
"	24 "		Patients admitted for week ending 24/3 " 112. Evacuated to 7 July 118. Remaining in Hosp. 6.	RTR

Army Form C. 2118.

WAR DIARY
or
INTELLIGENCE SUMMARY. 75 M - 7 d Unl.

(Erase heading not required.)

Instructions regarding War Diaries and Intelligence Summaries are contained in F. S. Regs., Part II. and the Staff Manual respectively. Title pages will be prepared in manuscript.

Place	Date	Hour	Summary of Events and Information	Remarks and references to Appendices
A.18.d.6.a Sh. 36.	31st March 1917		Cases admitted for week ending 31.3.17 6hr; 17 — twenigh + theveryes totaly 63. Remaining 8.	14.20

W. Davidson
Lt. Col. R.A.M.C.
o/c 75th F.A.

140/2066

25th Div.

A.D.M.S.

Obituary

COMMITTEE FOR THE
MEDICAL HISTORY OF THE WAR
Date -6 JUN 1917

WAR DIARY
or
INTELLIGENCE SUMMARY.

(Erase heading not required.)

Army Form C. 2118.

Vol 20

Place	Date	Hour	Summary of Events and Information	Remarks and references to Appendices
A.18.d.6.2 Sh 36.	2/4/17		Received orders to send 1 Officer 100 O.R's for work at T.B.C. O.P. Sht. 28, under O.C. 130 Coy. R.E., for construction of R.A.P. + A.D.S.	
"	4/17		Received R.A.M.C. order No. 60 15 (take over A.D.S. St. Quentin's Cabaret T.5.d.33 (Sh.28) from N.Z. 7.A. at 12 noon 6th April. Main body of Ambl. to remain at A.18.d.6.2.).	
"			Party sent to A.D.S. under Capt. O'Sullivan + Lt. Jones R.A.M.C.	
"	6/4/17		Cases admitted for week ending 7/4/17 70 discharged to duty or evacuated 69. Remanning trps. 15.	
"	7/4/17		Sick + wounded from A.D.S. are admitted direct to 77 F.A. at 13 Aillet L. Our trps. 75 F.A. at A.13.d.6.2 are to tan off. Work is being carried out on new A.D.S. at T.3.c.0.6 to R.A.P's at T.5.d.8.4 + N.35.d.7.2.	
"	14/4/17		Cases admitted for week ending 14th 68; evacuated or discharged to duty 45. Remanning in 14/4/17 28.5.	

2353 Wt. W3141/1454 700,000 5/15 D.D.&L. A.D.S.S./Form/C. 2118.

Army Form C. 2118.

WAR DIARY
or
INTELLIGENCE SUMMARY.   75th Fld Amb.
(Erase heading not required.)

Place	Date	Hour	Summary of Events and Information	Remarks and references to Appendices
A.16.d.6.2.	22nd Ap. 1917		Patients admitted for week ending 21st April '17 wounded 6, sickness & duty 73. Remaining 25.	(1917)
"	28-		" admitted for week ending 28th April '17. wounded 1, sickness & discharged duty, 62. Remains 21.	1:00
"	29th		The A.D.S. at T.3.c.0.5. has been camouflaged with roofs for general, officers, dressing room, & Wire sandbags, slightly dugouts for 54 stretcher cases also a place for our ambulance car, kitchens latrines & have also been finished. The Regimental aid post at T.5.d.8.1. & W.3.3.d.7.2. can also nearly finish. I am very slightly camouflaged with bricks. Accommodation for patients together as they are Walking wounds & reinforcements will be in Field Ambulance. A.D.S. in case of an advance. The R.A.P. at T.5.d.8. & is Lights if chester lights. Received 28th Div. order G 118/17, New Zealand Div. will relieve 25th Div. in the line by 6 p.m. 30th A.D.S. & working parties withdrawn from front-area on relief	f:00
"	30th			4 a.m.

I.P.C. Begaltson
75th F.A. Col R.A.M.C.

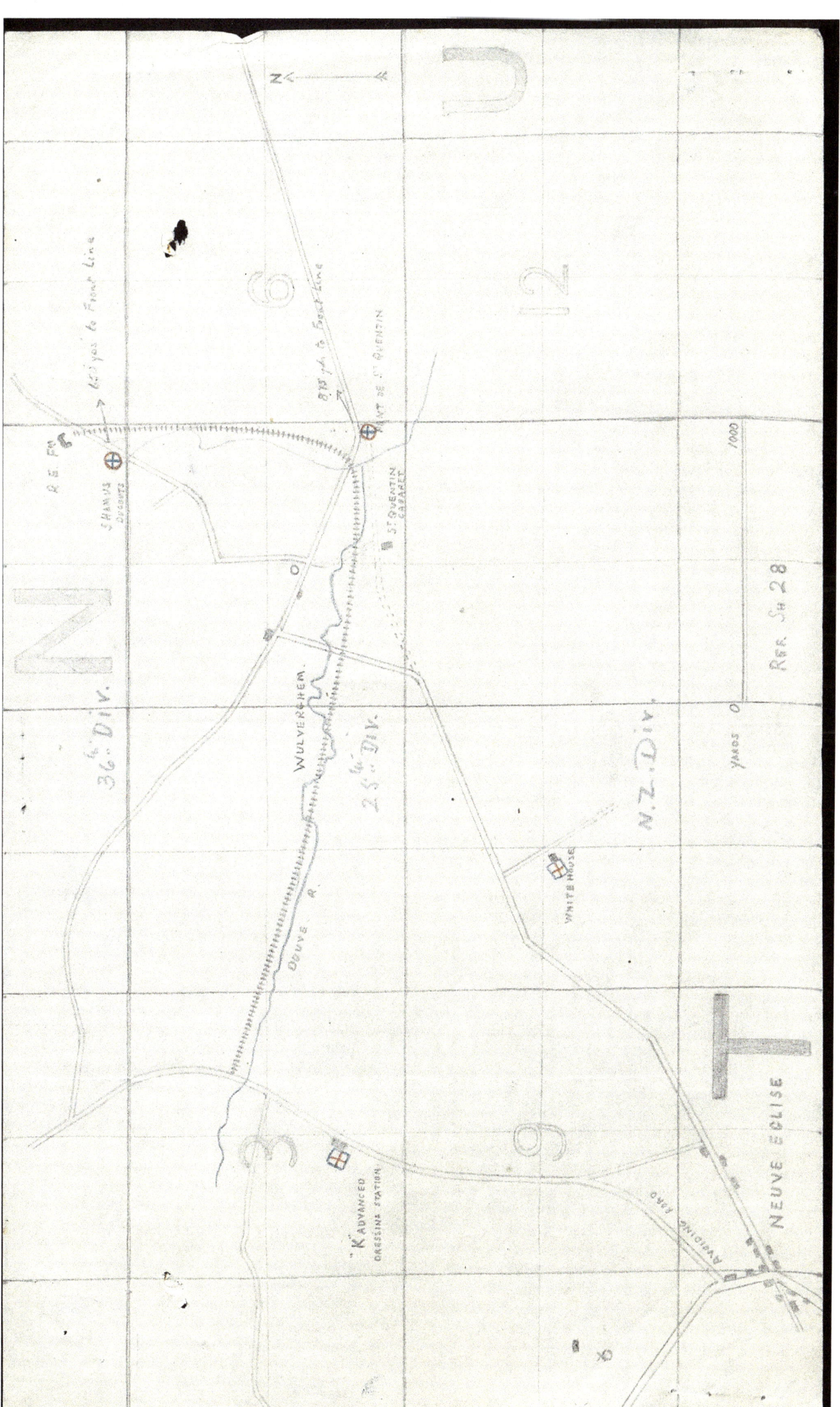

25th Divn

No. 75. 7.a.

COMMITTEE FOR THE
MEDICAL HISTORY OF THE WAR
Date 10 JUL. 1917

Army Form C. 2118.

WAR DIARY
or
INTELLIGENCE SUMMARY. 75th Amb
(Erase heading not required.)

Instructions regarding War Diaries and Intelligence Summaries are contained in F. S. Regs., Part II. and the Staff Manual respectively. Title pages will be prepared in manuscript.

Place	Date	Hour	Summary of Events and Information	Remarks and references to Appendices
A.gd.C.2 STEENWERCK	1/5/17		25th Div. Orders No. 113/7, Div. in Army Reserve from 24th, turnout at 36 hrs. notice. Still under administration of II ANZAC's. 75th F.A. Collecting sick of 74th Brigade in La CRECHE area, transport packed ready to move at for an possible.	
"	5/5/17		For week ending 5th May. Admissions 51. Evacuated 0. Discharged to duty 46. Remained 5.	11-10-30
"	8/5/17		Received R.A.M.C order No 64 that the 74th Brigade will relieve 1st N. Zealand Brig. by 3. a.m. May 11th in the WULVERGHEM Sector.	14000
"	10/5/17		Took over A.D.S. + Regtl Aid posts from N.Z. F.A. 'B' Section under Captain Huyshe att. Batt.	1700
"	12/5/17		For week ending May 12th admissions 4.5. Discharges 36; Remaining 26.	18-2-1
"	19/5/17		'C' Section Bearers + 'A' Section working in forward area under R.E. 'A' (2) Sub-div. Running Hospital at Hd. Qrs. A 18. d. 6.2. Admissions for week ending 19 b: 34; discharges 34; remaining 15; wounded sick + sick at A 13. d. 6. 2. wounded sick from Battalions in the line go to the Corps M.D. Station.	1700 / 1700

2353 Wt. W2514/1454 700,000 5/15 D.D.&L. A.D.S.S./Form/C. 2118.

Army Form C. 2118.

WAR DIARY
or
INTELLIGENCE SUMMARY. 75th :: F.A.

(Erase heading not required.)

Place	Date	Hour	Summary of Events and Information	Remarks and references to Appendices
A18.d.6.2	27/5/17		Admissions for week ending 26th May 32, evacuations & discharges 27. R.A.M.C. order No. 65. 7th Inf. Brig. Reorganizes 19. 75th F.A. remains as at present - but one section to accompany 74th Inf. Brig. to training ground at RECQUES. 'B' section details under Captain A.H. HUYCKE — Captain BENT marches on 24th from Hd. Qrs. to NORDPEENE. The men being carried in Horse Ambulance waggons. Remainder of Brigade went by train. 12 Animals + 1 C A.S.C. driver sent to D.H.Q R.A.M.C. order No. 66. Three kits used as pack animals by Division at R.A.M.C. order No. 67. 25th Div. Concentrate Sep 31." Ind.	
"	28/5/17			
"	30/5/17		Marches to TRAVECSBURG.	

HBDavidson
Lt. Col. R.A.M.C.

140/220

June 1917

No. 75. F.A.

COMMITTEE FOR THE
MEDICAL HISTORY OF THE WAR
Date - 7 AUG. 1917

WAR DIARY
or
INTELLIGENCE SUMMARY. 75th W. F.A.
(Erase heading not required.)

Army Form C. 2118.

Place	Date	Hour	Summary of Events and Information	Remarks and references to Appendices
RAVEISBURG	3/6/17	midnight	Raid carried out by 7th Brigade, 22 casualties passed thro' A.D.S. Prisoners captured by WORCESTERS.	
"	4th "		Raid by 7th Brigade (1st WILTS) few casualties.	
"K" A.D.S. T.3.d.0.4.	6th "		Received R.A.M.C. order No S.13.622 Medical Arrangements. O.C. 75th F.A. in charge of 3 Divisions of bearers & 15 Sunbeam cars. Summary of orders were:– 10 pier 27 V.P.'s at SHAMUS R.A.P. N.35.d.6.0.; 10 pier 27 O.P.'s at T.P.A.P. PONT ST-QUENTIN T.6.C.1.4; 32 O.R.s at CABARET ST QUENTIN, & Remainder of 75th F.A. at "K" A.D.S T.3.d.0.4. Casualties were taken from the R.A.P.s by wheeled stretcher to the CABARET where they were transferred to trolleys & (where daylight) railway to "K" A.D.S. There were 91 casualties before Zero. Runners were attached to each Brigade, & after the advance they enabled the F.A. to get into contact with the new R.A.P.s. The Bearer Division of 77 F.A. was himmed upon ready to advance at Zero to reinforce each of the R.A.P.s. Two bearer sub divisions of 76th F.A. were kept in reserve & went used later in the morning about 7am to reinforce PONT ST. QUENTIN. being open to PONT ST. QUENTIN a little late – to SHAMUS. About 9 am. these two parts were formed	
"	Zero 3.10 am			
"	7th "		By 7 A.M. cars were		

WAR DIARY
INTELLIGENCE SUMMARY. 75th F.A.

Army Form C. 2118.

Place	Date	Hour	Summary of Events and Information	Remarks and references to Appendices
T.3.d.0.4	7/u		formed into advanced dressing Stations. 76th F.A. took charge of Pont St. Quentin + Shamus remained in charge 78th F.A. The bearers were distributed as follows: Pont St. Quentin 76th F.A. bearer Div. + bearer Div. 177 F.A. Shamus 75th F.A. The advance was very rapid but it turned out to be nearly its reverse of what we had anticipated. Immediately after Zero the F.A. bearers advanced to the old British front line + assembly trenches + cleared the casualties, there being practically clear(?) no many land to get in contact with R.A.P.'s on either flank that had been established in the old German lines. More advanced posts were gradually pushed + two brigades were practically clear by midday. Most of the cases from this advance were got in by the end of the day. Relays were formed by the Regts + F.A. bearers + the evacuation worked very well.	

Army Form C. 2118.

WAR DIARY
or
INTELLIGENCE SUMMARY.   75 u. F.A.

(Erase heading not required.)

Instructions regarding War Diaries and Intelligence
Summaries are contained in F. S. Regs., Part II.
and the Staff Manual respectively. Title pages
will be prepared in manuscript.

Place	Date	Hour	Summary of Events and Information	Remarks and references to Appendices
B.D.S.	8th		Enemy bombardment & assault. Checked but apparently 2 Coys of 25th Div. casualties not numerous. Germans reinforced & came in advanced posts, all casualties cleared at that time as far as could be ascertained.	
"	"	9 am	⅓ of bearers withdrawn to "K" A.D.S. for rest & refill.	
"	"	11 am	11th Div. to take over from 25th Div.	
"	"	12 pm	Evacuates Sharius & "K" A.D.S. to take over 25th Div. next station BAILLEUL	
BAILLEUL	21st		R.A.M.C. order No 75. 25th Div. to be relieved by 3rd Aust. on 22/23rd. D.R.S. BAILLEUL to be handed over to 10th Aust. F.A.	
CAUDESCURE	23rd U		Marched at 2.30 p.m. arrived at CAUDESCURE 5.15 p.m.	
LE CORNET BRASSART	24		" 10 pm arrived LE CORNET BRASSART 3.30 a.m.	

Army Form C. 2118.

WAR DIARY
or
INTELLIGENCE SUMMARY. 75th F.A.
(Erase heading not required.)

Instructions regarding War Diaries and Intelligence Summaries are contained in F. S. Regs., Part II. and the Staff Manual respectively. Title pages will be prepared in manuscript.

Place	Date	Hour	Summary of Events and Information	Remarks and references to Appendices
LECORNET BRASSART	June 25th 1917		Marched 8 p.m.	
HUNINGHEM	26th		Arrived 1 a.m. Marched 8 p.m.	wao
LISBURG	26th		Arrived at LISBURG 10.30 p.m. 26th June. Took over billets + School as hospital, collecting field of 74th Brigade.	wao

H.Davidson
Lt. Col. R.F.A. ©
75th F.A.

COMMITTEE FOR THE
MEDICAL HISTORY OF THE WAR

Date 10 SEP. 1917

Confidential   July 1917

War Diary

Medical

75 F. Ambulance

Vol 23

WAR DIARY
INTELLIGENCE SUMMARY. 75th F.A.

Army Form C. 2118.

Place	Date	Hour	Summary of Events and Information	Remarks and references to Appendices
	8.7.17		R.A.M.C. order No 79, 75th & 74th F.A. to take over D.R.S. at L.23.a.5.7. from 26th F.A. on the 9/7/16. 1 enw are and Sub. div which will remain at LISBURG to collect Sub. div: proceeds advance H.Q.	
LISBURG	9.7.17		Captain A.H. HUGHES & B Sect Sub. div: proceeds advance H.Q.	
STEENVOORDE			Party & Cook over the D.R.S. main body & transport proceeded to STEENVOORDE	
			" " L.23.a.5.7 (REMY SIDING) H.Q.	
REMY SIDING	10.7.17 14.7.17		Hospital return for week ending Saturday 14.7.17. admitted officers 3, transferred from 26th F.A. 13 discharged to 64th & C.C.S.2. Other ranks admitted 93, (transferred from 26th F.A. 230. " 76th " 82. " 41st C.C.S. 9.	
	22.7.17		Received R.A.M.C. order No 82. to hand over D.R.S. to 2nd F.A. on 2nd. Divisions in vicinity of REMY SIDING. Received "Z" Scheme of Medical Operations for II Corps. D.R.9 handed over to 75th F.A. Received S.B. 782, 75th F.A. in event of hostile offensive action by the Bn. will remain in field unless ordered otherwise by the Div. at LANDBOUVER F.A.Pn, from 25.7.17.	map map

Army Form C. 2118.

WAR DIARY
or
INTELLIGENCE SUMMARY. 75th F.A.
(Erase heading not required.)

Place	Date	Hour	Summary of Events and Information	Remarks and references to Appendices
REMY SIDING	24/7		In accordance with G 27/725, 6 pack animals sent to Divisional Pack Transport Company, instead of 8 as ⅓ of the transport is with 74th Brigade Group.	
LANDBOUVER FARM	25/7/17		Took over LANDBOUVER FARM G.21.b.2.2. (Sheet 28. 1-40,000) Received orders to send one tent sub-div. to Army Rest Camp (with two Officers) at St MOMELINS, to arrive by 26th. Diverted this tent sub-div marching with 74th Brigade for this duty. They had arrived at GODEWAERSVELDE. Arrangements being made to collect the sick of the Brigade from H.Q. G.S. R.A.M.C. orders 83 & 84 to send to pack animal H.20.a.5-5-t t move to VANSCHIER FARM cancelled. M.V. 2249. The Brigadier R.A.M.C. order No 85. 75th F.A. to collect sick from 7th Brigade.	H & W
17-20
H & W
H & W
	26/7/17		No 86. 75th F.A. will attach 1 M.O. & 50 bearers to 76th F.A. & 1 M.O. & 50 bearers to 77th F.A.; one stretcher bearer to be sent & 7 wheeled stretchers, in y morning. 75th F.A. to take over VANSCHIER FARM and DR.S along with LANDBOUVET FARM.	H & W
	28/7/17		Ambulances to be sent to 8th Div. when called for. Took over VANSCHIER FARM from 76th F.A. with 30 particulars. Bearers sent to join 76th & 77th F.A's	H & W
	30 4.			H & W

Army Form C. 2118.

WAR DIARY
or
INTELLIGENCE SUMMARY.
(Erase heading not required.)

Instructions regarding War Diaries and Intelligence Summaries are contained in F. S. Regs., Part II. and the Staff Manual respectively. Title pages will be prepared in manuscript.

Place	Date	Hour	Summary of Events and Information	Remarks and references to Appendices
VANSOHIER FARM	30.17		4 Sunbeams to report at Gate B=L45 H 29.b.8.5 (Sheet 28) by 6 a.m. 31st. 75th F.A. klape in N.Y.D.N Cases returned from 62 C.C.S. D.R.S to be closed by 9 A.M. 31st.	
	31st		D.R.S closed.	

H.A.Davidson
Lt-Col. R.A.M.C
75th F.A.

Volume 23

Confidential

August 14th

War Diary

Medical
75th F. Ambulance
25th Division

August 1917

140/2364

Vol 24

WAR DIARY
or
INTELLIGENCE SUMMARY.

(Erase heading not required.)

Army Form C. 2118.

Place	Date	Hour	Summary of Events and Information	Remarks and references to Appendices
VANSOHIER FARM G.21.c.5.7 Sheet 28.	8/17		R.A.M.C. order No. 90. 75th F.A. to have open LANDBOUYER FARM to 24th F.A. & transport. Hd. Qrs. to VANSOHIER FARM, which will be 25th Div. D.R.S.	(nod)
	4/8		A.D.M.S. No S.T. 75th F.A. to collect sick from reserve brigade. Captain LINDSAY sent to 2 R.I.R. in place of Lt. (?) F. W. R. Kms. Killed.	(nod)
	6/8		Received R. Km. @ O.O. No 91, attack to be made on Saillbeaux and S) Westhoek ridge.	
			R.A.M.C. order No 91, 74th Brigade to take WESH OEK wood.	(nod)
	10/8		" " 92 relating to relief's of casualties.	(nod)
	11		" " 93 " " STEENVOORDE Area.	
			75th F.A. collect sick from STEENVOORDE Area.	
	12		R.M.C. O.O. 9 h relating to relief of right sector by 86th Dis. relief to be completed by 10 a.m. 13th Aug.	
			R.A.M.C. O.O. 95. Relief ?) Div. on left by 8th Div. ?- on Bl. Rly. 56th Div. to be completed by 10 a.m. 14th. Dis ?-	(nod)
	13		Captain Stephenson + Captain O'Sullivan theaar Div. report at Hd. Qrs. having handed over Birr & Rds. to always kept on Rd. section Railway woo advanced posts on left respectively. These Offices were completed under covenous of O.O. 76th F.A.	(nod)

Army Form C. 2118.

WAR DIARY
or
INTELLIGENCE SUMMARY. 75th F.A.

(Erase heading not required.)

Place	Date	Hour	Summary of Events and Information	Remarks and references to Appendices
VANSCHIER FARM C.21.C.5.7.	14th Aug.		During period 1st to 14th Aug. admissions to D.R.S. were as follows:— Officers 2.5- to C.C.S 20 to 2nd Corps D.R.S. 5. O.R's 948 to C.C.S. 342 to duty 515.	
"	15th		Received T.R.M.C. order No. 96. 75th F.A. to collect sick from 112th F.A., R.F.A. Curragh Camp. 25th Div. Lowa artillery & 75th F.A. & 198 Coy. R.E. to be withdrawn to the STEENVOORDE & EECKE area. 75th F.A. to remain in D.R.S. (R.A.M.C. order No 97).	
"	16th			
"	18th		R.A.M.C. order No 98 – 7th Brigade group from Steenvoorde to Dominion Camp (less 77th F.A. & R.F. Coy), 75th F.A. to collect sick of 7th Brigade. R.A.M.C. order No 99, collection of sick own order No 98.	
"	19th			
"	21st		25th Div. O. No 223, 6th S.W. Borderers to Belgian Chateau Area sick to be collected by 75th F.A.	
"	23rd		LANDROUVER FARM handed over to F.A. 23rd Div. all equipment transferred to VINSCHIER FARM. 112th Bde. R.F.A. to G/18.C. Sh. 28. Sick to be collected by 75th F.A.	
"	24th		110th " " " " " " " "	
"	28th			

2353 Wt. W2344/1454 700,000 5/15 D.D.&L. A.D.S.S./Forms/C. 2118.

WAR DIARY
or
INTELLIGENCE SUMMARY.   75th. T.A.

(Erase heading not required.)

Army Form C. 2118.

Place	Date	Hour	Summary of Events and Information	Remarks and references to Appendices
VANSOHIER FARM C.21.C.5.7 Sh. 28	31.8.17		Material has been drawn for the erection of a dining room for the patients & for an extension of the hall house & work is proceeding on these buildings. Three marquees have been drawn from C.M.D.S. & erected.	

HADavidson
Lt. Col. R.A.M.C.
75th. T.A.

VOLUME 24.

SEPTEMBER 1917.

"WAR DIARY"

MEDICAL

CONFIDENTIAL

75th FIELD AMBULANCE.

R. A. M. C.

Army Form C. 2118.

WAR DIARY
or
INTELLIGENCE SUMMARY. 75th F.A.
(Erase heading not required.)

Instructions regarding War Diaries and Intelligence Summaries contained in F. S. Regs., Part II. and the Manual respectively. Title pages will be prepared in manuscript.

Place	Date	Hour	Summary of Events and Information	Remarks and references to Appendices
VANSOMER FARM.	1/9/17		R.A.M.C. order No 101 — 74th + 75th Bdes. to DOMINION + OUDERDOM areas. Zero actions 106th F.Coy R.E. to H.2.a.L + KRUISSTRAAT, 2nd F.A. collection to 75th F.A.	(?AD)
"	2/9/17		R.A.M.C. order No 102 — 25th Div. to take over front of 23rd Div. 75th Adv/fort-7.37 D.H.Q + railhead DICKEBUSCH. 75th F.A. remain at VANSCHIER — 76th to take over M-line — 77th F.A. are M/PA. R.A.M.C. order No 103 — IInd Corps transfers to 2nd Army — Now 3rd Corps medical scheme ceases + Naval Div. medical arrangements to be carried out. 75th F.A. to take over WARATAH Camp as D.R.S, stretcher bearing party at VISHER. 76th F.A. in line. 77th F.A. main dressing station. 25th Div. No A.2.443 — 4 animals + drivers to be sent to Pack transport, to[?] at "K" dump. 7th Brigade to Div. relieve in place of 75th Bde., 75th F.A. to collect them with. 1 M.O. + lino heaven ded—dio.s to report to O.C. 76th F.A. 2nd. at DAS. MENIN ROAD 6 p.m. 4th Sept. Captain C.J. SULLIVAN R.A.M.C. went in command of the bearers.	(AD) (AD)
"	3/9/17			(AD)
"	4/9/17			(AD)
"	7/9/17		15th am WARATAH By 11 a.m. Received R.A.M.C. order No 105 — 25th Div. to be relieved by 47th Div. by 10 a.m. 10th Sept. 75th F.A. to hand over WARATAH to No 7 F.A. 2nd Aust: Div. on Sept. 9th + to collect sick from 74th Brigade.	(AD)

Army Form C. 2118.

WAR DIARY
or
INTELLIGENCE SUMMARY. 75th 2 F.A.
(Erase heading not required.)

Place	Date	Hour	Summary of Events and Information	Remarks and references to Appendices
WARATAH CAMP D.R.S.	8th Sept. 1917		Captain C.J. SULLIVAN R.A.M.C returned with bearers & 1 N.C.O. 1 8 men.	
			Received 25th Div. Order No. 288: 25th Div. transferred to 1st Army 1st Corps & proceed to the AUCHEL area.	
	9th		1 Section 7th F.A. 2nd Aus. Div. arrived to take over D.R.S.	
	10th		Received G.113. Troops of 74th Brigade to Entrain at G.29.b. Central.	
			At 2:30 p.m., delivering parcel CAESTRE.	
			Brigade transport to march to CAESTRE area.	
			R.A.M.C order No 106 reference March Route from 2nd Army to 1st Army to AUCHEL area.	
CAESTRE	11th		Arrived CAESTRE & occupied a Camp near the village.	
"	12th		Marched to STEENBECQUE area, under 74th Brigade orders.	
THIENNE	13		Marched to AUCHEL area.	
AUCHEL	14th		Billets & Hospital in Hotel de Ville AUCHEL.	
"	24th		Received R.A.M.C order No 107. 25th Division to take over from 6th Division front area from N.13.b.6.0 to N.8.c.7.0. 75th Brigade Group to relieve 71st Brigade. 76th - 74. to take over M.D.S at- R.8 Central Franc 10. Ref. Maps 36 b etc.	

WAR DIARY or INTELLIGENCE SUMMARY

Army Form C. 2118.

75th" F.A.

Place	Date	Hour	Summary of Events and Information	Remarks and references to Appendices
AUEUIL	April 28 17		75th Brigade group is placed under command of G.O.C 6th Div. Amendment to R.A.M.C. order 107. Div. Hd. Qrs. remain at La BOUVRIERE.	

H.A. Davidson
Lt. Col. R.M.C.

Volume 25

Confidential

War Diary

Medical

75th F. Ambulance

October 1917

Army Form C. 2118.

WAR DIARY
or
INTELLIGENCE SUMMARY.   75th Field Amb

(Erase heading not required.)

Place	Date	Hour	Summary of Events and Information	Remarks and references to Appendices
AUCHEL C.27.b.8.3	3/10/17	4 p.m.	Received B.M.O 479 from 74th Inf. Brigade - units to move to unknown part of line on morning of 4th.	
		9 p.m.	74th Brigade order No 148 - Brigade to march on 4th Oct to area ANEZIN - BETHUNE barracks - to relieve 99th Inf. Brigade in the CAMBRIN Sector on 5th & fortnight of 5th/6th.	
"	4/10/17		Marched out at 10.25 a.m. & arrived at BETHUNE Barracks around noon.	14-20
BETHUNE E.5.a.3.0.	5/10/17	2 p.m.	Received R.A.M.C. order No 108 & additions to these orders. In accordance with R.A.M.C. order No.108 an advance party proceeded to take over the CAMBRIN Sector from the 6th F.A. 2nd Division. The R.A.M.C. bearers in the R.A.P's were relieved in the morning & the A.D.S. at CAMBRIN was taken over in the afternoon. The A.D.S. at Harley St. and bearers in Canal Sector to the latter area on 6th. Part of the ECOLE CATERIVE, BETHUNE was fitted up as an M.D.S. The evacuation of the right Divisional sector is as follows:- Main Dressing Station - ECOLE CATERIVE - BETHUNE (E.5.a.3.0.) Advanced " " S - HARLEY STREET - A.20.d.4.9 } Bethune - CAMBRIN - A.26.a.1.5 } Cambrin Sect. R.A.P's - Southern half of Canal Sector. HARTFORD St. reserve aid post A.21.a.5.7	14-20

Army Form C. 2118.

WAR DIARY
or
INTELLIGENCE SUMMARY. 75th Field Ambulance &c.

(Erase heading not required.)

Instructions regarding War Diaries and Intelligence Summaries are contained in F. S. Regs., Part II. and the Staff Manual respectively. Title pages will be prepared in manuscript.

Place	Date	Hour	Summary of Events and Information	Remarks and references to Appendices
BETHUNE E.9.a.3.0.			Montrail Evacuation from Headpost St. R.A.P. by trench or by wheeled stretcher down mountain House road. (approximate distance 600 yds.) ROBERTSON'S ALLEY R.A.P. A.27.a.6.4. Right Batt. Canal Sector – Evacuation by hand ROBERTSON'S ALLEY – WILSON'S WAY & thence by hand tramway to HARLEY St. CAMBRIN SECTOR R.A.P's. Guy's post – HUMANITY Trench – by day evacuation by trench RAILWAY ALLEY to CAMBRIN. (map ref. Guy's G.3.a.3.9.) At night the broad gauge railway can be used to relay post at BRAYS KEEP. From BRAYS KEEP to A.D.S. by wheeled stretcher or motor Ambulance. Distance from BRAYS KEEP to R.A.P 1600 yds. & from relay post to A.D.S. 1000 yds. Cambrin Sector night aid post:– BARTS (G.9.a.3.9) Evacuation by trench or wheeled stretcher to A.D.S. at VERMELLES approximate distance 1000 yds. This A.D.S belongs to the 46th Div & a sunbeam car is stationed there to clear cases belonging to [illegible] 25th Div.	R.A.O

2333 Wt. W3544/1454 700,000 5/15 D. D. & L. A.D.S.S./Forms/C. 2118.

Army Form C. 2118.

WAR DIARY
or
INTELLIGENCE SUMMARY 75th Field Ambulance

(Erase heading not required.)

Instructions regarding War Diaries and Intelligence Summaries are contained in F. S. Regs., Part II. and the Staff Manual respectively. Title pages will be prepared in manuscript.

Place	Date	Hour	Summary of Events and Information	Remarks and references to Appendices
BETHUNE	1st Oct		Received employed in forward area 2 Officers 60 O.R's. 4 O.R's attached to each R.A.P. remainder at the various A.D. Stations — HARLEY St. is mainly used as A.D.S. CAMBRIN being held by a body which are M.O. in addition one Sunbeam + one Ford car are stationed at HARLEY St. + one Sunbeam car at VERMELLES.	
	4th		5th & 11th Batts. S. Staffs. 5th Brig. C.E.P. to the trenches + 74th & 2/3 Brigade for training. 2.5th Div. in dev. 23s.	
	5th Oct		4th Batt. S. Staffordshire Regt. joins 2.5th Div. 13th O. etr. Sick the collected by 75th Field Ambulance.	
	22nd		Transport line's changed to E.4. Central. Bethune Cavalrie Reft. Received instructions for evacuation in case of heavy shelling in	
	28th		BETHUNE. Ambulances to move into ROBECQ, P.23.d, to open two receptions of sick wounded, guard to the left at FERRE CATERIVE.	
	31st		M.D.S. inspected by the D.D.M.S. XI Corps.	

A.A. Davidson
Lt. Col. R.A.M.C.
75th Field Ambulance.

Vol. 26 Confidential

War Diary

Medical

75th F Ambulance

November 1917

WAR DIARY
INTELLIGENCE SUMMARY. 75th Field Ambulance.

Army Form C. 2118.

Place	Date	Hour	Summary of Events and Information	Remarks and references to Appendices
BETHUNE E.s.Q.S.O.			Evacuation of sick – BART's R.A.P. VERMELLES SEBS – a car as rest men kept at the 46th Div. A.D.S., the 97 C.O. & one man have been withdrawn & one man left as messenger, in case a car or assistance is required from HARLEY St. A.R.S. The position of BRAYS Kef relay post has been changed to a safer place under the railway, about two yds further however position	(encl)
"	22nd/17	4 p.m.	XI Corps Hd. Qrs. will be relieved by XV Corps Hd. Qrs. at 4 p.m. today, 22nd Nov.	(encl)
"	23rd/17		25th Div. No. G.113 d – detachments of 7d. Cys R.E., D.W. B's + detachments of Inf. Brigades to proceed to PETIGNY–LISBOURG – To M.y. on 24th Nov. to 1st Army training area, came with the heaters in 7d. Aml. es of Canadian Division. 75th F.A. to collect sick from transport of above on the 25th at HAUT RIEUX & BAS RIEUX.	(encl)
"	25th		R.A.M.E. order 90110, 25th Div. to be relieved by 42nd Div. in GIVENCHY & CANAL SECTORS & by 46th Div. in the CAMBRIN SECTOR, from Nov. 27th & 28th, 2nd and 3rd Bdes, 3rd.	(encl)

WAR DIARY or INTELLIGENCE SUMMARY

Army Form C. 2118.

75th - 7th Fd. Amb.

Place	Date	Hour	Summary of Events and Information	Remarks and references to Appendices
BETHUNE	27/11/17		Amendment to R.A.M.C. order 110, 75th & 7th Ambces will remain - ECOLE CATOTIVE BETHUNE will be under orders of 42nd Div. from 12 noon 28th Nov. 75th & 7th Ambces will arrange to collect sick from 125th Bris. in Bethune area on 28th & 126th Brigade on 29th Nov.	
	29/11/17		A.D.M.S. S/231 on 2/3rd Dec. 25th Div. Artillery (less portion covering Cambrin Sector) moves to GONNEHEM, FOUQUEREUIL, HESDIGNEUL areas. 74th Inf. Brigade marches from CAMBRIN area to area South of BETHUNE. 75th Field Ambulance will collect their sick.	

H.A. Trenidian,
Lt. Col. R.A.M.C.

Volume 26   December 1917

75th Field Ambulance
R.A.M.C

War Diary

Medical

Confidential

Army Form 2118.

WAR DIARY
or
INTELLIGENCE SUMMARY. 75th Field Ambulance.
(Erase heading not required.)

Instructions regarding War Diaries and Intelligence Summaries are contained in F. S. Regs., Part II. and the Staff Manual respectively. Title pages will be prepared in manuscript.

Place	Date	Hour	Summary of Events and Information	Remarks and references to Appendices
BETHUNE ECOLE CATORIVE	1/12/17		Division is held in readiness to move by rail from 1st Corps Area to 3rd Army, to commence about noon 3rd December.	Intro
"	"		74th Brigade A.B/S.15. On relief by 42nd Div. 75th F.A. will go to ANNEZIN.	mm(ii)
"	"		R.A.M.C. order No 111. 75th F.A. will move under orders of G.O.C. 74th Inf. Brig. on 2nd to ANNEZIN. 75th F.A. will hand over ECOLE CATORIVE & A.D.S. HARLEY St. to a Field Ambulance of 42nd Div., & A.D.S. CAMBRIN to a Fld. Ambulance of 46th Division.	
ANNEZIN	2/12/17		Handed over to-day & marched to ANNEZIN at 3.30 p.m. & took over Hospital + "billets" in ANNEZIN. Received R.A.M.C. order No 112, 26th Div. to be transferred from 1st Army to 3rd Army on 3rd December. Move to be by rail entrainment to start by rail. day 3rd December, on detrainment Division to be accommodated in AEHIET area. C.C.S. or Stationary Hospital. Sick to be evacuated to nearest	mm(iv)

Army Form C. 2118.

WAR DIARY
or
INTELLIGENCE SUMMARY. 75th Bde Hd. Art.ee

(Erase heading not required.)

Instructions regarding War Diaries and Intelligence Summaries are contained in F. S. Regs., Part II. and the Staff Manual respectively. Title pages will be prepared in manuscript.

Place	Date	Hour	Summary of Events and Information	Remarks and references to Appendices
ANNEZIN	3/12/17		25th Div. Instructions – 75th F.A. to entrain with 74th Brigade group at CHOCQUES morning of Dec. 6th. 6th Div. detrain at ACHIET-LE-GRAND & the accommodated at a point from ACHIET-LE-GRAND – LIGEAST PARK. Rations to be carried for 4th + 5th. Supply wagons to accompany unit. 1 M.O. + Ambulance Car to attend entraining of Artillery at BETHUNE + detraining at BEISSEUX-AU-MONT.	(1&2)
	3/12/17		Instructions for move of 74th Brigade to 3rd Army area. 75th F.A. to entrain at CHOCQUES – time of train 7.52 a.m. 5th Dec. 1 N.C.O. as billeting party to go on 11.52 p.m. train on 4th Dec. Transport to arrive at station 3 hrs before time of departure. Personnel 1½ hrs before. Brig. Q. established places to act as loading party. Zinc blankets per man to be carried.	(3)
			Received B.M.O. 171 – The Division is under 1 hrs. notice to move. 74th Inf. Brigade. The Brigade will move early tomorrow & march to	
ACHIET-LE-GRAND	5/12/17		R.A.M. Order No. 112 – 25th Div. less Artillery this transfers from VI Corps to V Corps on Dec. 6th & move to V Corps area, D.L.P.n.S. GREVILLERS.	
"	"		74th Brigade Order No. 164 – Brigade group will march to BEAULENCOURT AREA on Dec. 6th.	(4&5)

2353 Wt. W2544/1454 700,000 5/15 D. D. & L. A.D.S.S./Forms/C. 2118.

Army Form C. 2118.

WAR DIARY
or
INTELLIGENCE SUMMARY. 75th Fld. Amb.

(Erase heading not required.)

Instructions regarding War Diaries and Intelligence Summaries are contained in F. S. Regs., Part II. and the Staff Manual respectively. Title pages will be prepared in manuscript.

Place	Date	Hour	Summary of Events and Information	Remarks and references to Appendices
ACHIET-LE-GRAND.	6/12/17		R.A.M.C. order No. 113 - The 25th Div. will be placed at the disposal of VII Corps to take over a portion of 3rd Army front. 74th Brigade GROUP will move on 6th Dec. to Arras area of 3rd Div. at FAVREUIL where it will come under the orders of C.O. 3rd Div.	
	"		B.M.O. 200/1 74th Brigade Group will move to FAVREUIL field Ambulance passing the Starting point at 10.20 a.m.	
	"		Arrived at FAVREUIL & occupied huts on the FAVREUIL-MORY Road.	
FAVREUIL	7/12/17		74th Inf. Brigade will relieve 9th Inf. Brigade night of 7th & 8th Dec. Two Batts. in line + a third in intermediate line. Brigade Hd. Qrs. C.29.a. O.C. 75th F.A. will make arrangements for evacuation of those three Batts. in the line & will relieve 9th F.A. in that part of their by 11 p.m. on 7th Dec. No 3 F.A. will be responsible for A.D.S. at - at C.25.a. Authority, Operation order No 68 A.D.M.S. 3rd Division.	
	8/12/17		The 7th & 9th Inf. Brigade will take over the line held by 9th Inf. Brig., on night of 9th & 10th Dec. from front D.13.d.8.1. to C.1.2.a.4.3. 75th F.A. and the arrangement of loading 3rd Div. will collect from front held by 7th & 9th Inf. Brigade.	

Army Form C. 2118.

WAR DIARY
or
INTELLIGENCE SUMMARY.

(Erase heading not required.)

75th Brit: 7th H. A. C. Sanit Sec.

Place	Date	Hour	Summary of Events and Information	Remarks and references to Appendices
FAVREUIL	8/12/17		Moved from No 5 Camp to No 7 at 12.30 p.m. & from No 7 to No 6 Camp at 7.15 p.m. on 8th Dec.	
"	9/12/17		Moved from No 6 Camp to Field Ambulance site occupied by No 7 Field Ambulance at H.16.d.7.5. Received O. Order No 89, A.D.M.S. 3rd Division, 7.5–4– 2.A. on night of 9/10th Dec. relieving a.e. No 8 F.A. at A.D.S. at C.29.B.5.0. & be responsible for evacuation of 95th Divl. units in the Line.	
"	10/12/17		Took over evacuation of Line from No 8 F.A. Amb. A.D.S. at C.29.a.5.0. Personnel 2 officers 68 men, 8 bearers at each aid post, situated as follows:- C.23.b.8.8.; N.2 C.26.d.9.5.; No.3. D.26.c.1.3.; Support at C.30.a.5.8; Evacuation by hand carry to A.D.S. In addition Ambulance cars can reach No 3 post & wheeled stretchers could be used from No 2 to No 3.	
"	12/12/17		Divisional Hd. Qrs will close at GREVILLERS at 12 noon and re-14" hopen at Vis monument FAVREUIL 4.15.c. at same hour.	

Army Form 2118.

WAR DIARY
or
INTELLIGENCE SUMMARY. 75th. 4th Fd. Amb ee.

(Erase heading not required.)

Instructions regarding War Diaries and Intelligence Summaries are contained in F. S. Regs., Part II. and the Staff Manual respectively. Title pages will be prepared in manuscript.

Place	Date	Hour	Summary of Events and Information	Remarks and references to Appendices
FAVREUIL Camp No 16	12/12/17		The Left Div. boundary in forward area will be extended to C.5.d.8.0 hoot. C.5./1, H.6 & R.T. exclusive inclusive to 25th Division to present boundary at C.16. a.6.9. 75th Fd Amb. will arrange for evacuation. New area. Arrangements have been made to evacuate the areas through R.A.P. at C.11. a.7.2 through Amb. of 3rd Division via NOREUIL.	
"	14/12/17		The 25th Div. will be transferred from VI Corps to IV Corps about noon 15th Dec. R.A.M.C. Order No. 116, 75th & 7 Amb. will take over from 7th F. Amb. by Noon 15th Dec. 77th F. Amb. will take over from 142nd F.Amb.	
"	15/12/17		76th F.Amb. will take over Corps Rest Station BIHUCOURT. " " " " maintain holding party at SAPIGNIES. 75th " " " take over whole of No. 16 Camp.	
"	"		Field Ambulances will open for reception of sick & slightly wounded. 77th F.A. will detail 1 M.O. & supernumary personnel to A.D.S.	
"	21/12/17		at VAULX for the evacuation of cases from left sector of 25th Division front.	

Army Form C. 2118.

WAR DIARY
or
INTELLIGENCE SUMMARY.

(Erase heading not required.)

W.D. 2/4 Australian [?]

Place	Date	Hour	Summary of Events and Information	Remarks and references to Appendices
FAVREUIL	22/12/17		Sites for new A.D. posts have been selected on the right - near the road at D.26.c.0.24 - on the LANGICOURT - VAULX Road. @ 17.A.1.1. Working parties are to be provided for final from 75th 2/h of 9th Wessex from 77th F.A.	H.D
	27/12/17		Work commenced on new R.A.P's. A new deep dug-out to supplement the dressing room at a.D.S has been partly constructed & is being continued.	

H.A. Davidson
Lt. Col. R.A.M.C.
O.C. 75th Fld. Amb.

2353 Wt. W2544/1454 700,000 5/15 D. D. & L. A.D.S.S./Forms/C. 2118.

No. 75. 7. a.

Army Form C. 2118.

WAR DIARY
or
INTELLIGENCE SUMMARY.

75th Field Amb &c

Vol 29

(Erase heading not required.)

Instructions regarding War Diaries and Intelligence Summaries are contained in F.S. Regs., Part II. and the Staff Manual respectively. Title pages will be prepared in manuscript.

Place	Date	Hour	Summary of Events and Information	Remarks and references to Appendices
FAVREUIL 14.16.d.8.6.	8/1/19		75th F.A. to see sick of 105th F. Coy R.E at A.O.S. C.29.a.3.0.	16.00
"	10/1/18		75th F.A. will see sick of 1Cd. Qrs. of 75th + 195th M.G.C.B	11.00
"	12/1/18		75th Inf. Brigade will relieve 7th Inf. Brigade in the left sector during Jan 14th together of 14th, 15th.	11.00
"	23/1/18		The 7th Inf Brigade will relieve 75th Inf. Brig. in left sector of Div. front during Jan 28th, relief to be complete by 6 am on Jan. 27th.	11.20
"	24/1/18		25th Div. Signal School, necessity re situated at OVILLIN. 76th F.A. to detail M.O. on duty + 75th F.A. to detail 2nd carts to deal with the cases, sick to No 3 Sta. Hosp. DOULLENS. Inspec. + S.I. wounds to 58 C.O.S, EDGEHILL. On night of 26th Jan. machine gun Coys. 3 in line + 1 reserve. 74th M.G.C. in reserve.	11.00 14.00
"	25/1/18		76th Field Amb. to send Ford Amb. cars for duty at 25th Div. School OVILLIN.	14.00

HADavidson Lt. Col. R.M.C
75th Fd. Amb.

Volume XXVIII

Confidential

February 1918

War Diary

Medical

75 F Ambulance

WAR DIARY
or
INTELLIGENCE SUMMARY.

Army Form C. 2118.

75th Field Amb[ulance]

Place	Date	Hour	Summary of Events and Information	Remarks and references to Appendices
H.16.d.8.6.	2/1/18		Work done in forward area large dug-out completed 2nd A.D.S. at LAGNICOURT. size about 30ft by 7ft, over 20ft of head cover. Stretcher racks put up for 24 cases with room for walking cases in addition. Their dug-out communicates with the dressing room & has been made entirely by men of the unit. Most of the sand bagging at the A.D.S. has been renewed. Duckboards relaid & a kitchen dugout room & store completed. A new R.A.P. has been constructed about D.28.8.02. by R.H.M.L. Latrines, with R.E. supervision, other R.A.P.s near a road & in (aye?) an obvious target, be used as an A.D.S. The dressing room & space for patients measures 42' by 8' with racks for 18 stretcher cases & in addition accommodation is being provided for stretcher bearers. There are two latrines dug-outs for carrying stretchers to the head cover is over 20ft.	

WAR DIARY or INTELLIGENCE SUMMARY

Army Form C. 2118.

75th Fld. Amb.

Place	Date	Hour	Summary of Events and Information	Remarks and references to Appendices
H.16.d.8.6.	7/2/19	3.45	S. of 7/2/18 warning order ourl- to be relieved by 18th F.A. To move with Mob. Equipment except that 200 stretchers will be taken + 200 additional blankets. 25th Div. less Artillery to be relieved by 6th Div. (will move into ACHIET Area (R.A.M.C. operation order No. 119). R.A.P.'s right Brigade to be handed over to 18th F.A. by 75th F.A. on 11/2. M.D.S. FAVREUIL to be handed over by noon on 12th. A.D.S. LAGNICOURT + R.A.P.'s Left Brigade to be handed over on night of 12/13th, relief to be completed by 10 a.m. 13th.	
"	9/2/19		75th F.A. to take over aid accepted by 1/2 Highland F.A. at HERMIES-LE-GRAND. Unit to march independently. Sick offering ads to be collected.	

Army Form C. 2118.

WAR DIARY
or
INTELLIGENCE SUMMARY.
(Erase heading not required.)

Instructions regarding War Diaries and Intelligence Summaries are contained in F. S. Regs., Part II. and the Staff Manual respectively. Title pages will be prepared in manuscript.

Place	Date	Hour	Summary of Events and Information	Remarks and references to Appendices
H.16.d.6.6	12/7/18		Handed over R.M. Brigade aid posts to 16th Field Ambulance + M.D.S. FAVREUIL. Marched at 1 p.m. to ACHIET-LE-GRAND took over ambulance site from 1/2nd Highland Fd. Amb.	
ACHIET.LE. GRAND	13/7/18		Handed over A.D.S. LAGNICOURT + left Brigade R.A.P's to 18th Field Amb.	
"	23/7/18		Unit inspected by G.O.C. 2nd Division	
"	27/7/18		Unit inspected by D.M.S. 3rd Army	

H.R.Davidson
Lt. Col. R.A.M.C.
75th Fd. Amb.

A.D.S.S./Form/C. 2118.

Volume 30   March 1918

Confidential

War Diary

Medical

75th Field Ambulance

R.A.M.C.

Vol 31
140/902

Army Form C. 2118.

WAR DIARY
or
INTELLIGENCE SUMMARY.
(Erase heading not required.)

Place	Date	Hour	Summary of Events and Information	Remarks and references to Appendices
ACHIET- LE-GRAND RITZ Camp	3/3/18		Received warning order No. G.S. 278. 25th Div. to relieve 6th Div. in the line on 12th to 7th March. leaves M.C. Butt. 75th F.A. to take over D.R.S. at B + PIGNIES. Received Corps defence scheme.	
"	5/3/18 (?)		Relief by 25th Div. notified in No. G.S. 278 is confirmed. Received 25th Div. Medical defence scheme in the event of active operations by the enemy. 1. 6th Div. moves up in support on present IV Corps front. 2. 26th Div. takes over present 6th Div. front. 75th F.A. 14th Qrs. would be at I 26. b. 5.6 (57c N.W.1 zone) with evidence of Bourin Division. 77th F.A. would clear casualties if not brigaded on right. Corps main Dressing Station for stretcher cases would be at BEUGNY – 77th F.A. in charge of walking wounded.	M.D.

WAR DIARY or INTELLIGENCE SUMMARY
Army Form C. 2118.

75th Field Ambulance

Place	Date	Hour	Summary of Events and Information	Remarks and references to Appendices
N° 4 IGT-LE-GRAND RITZ CAMP	7/3/18		25th Div. order No 278. Amendment. 74th Brigade will be prepared to arrange by heavy cut ropes and also dismounted portions 575 to 7th Nov. The Mounted portion will move at Zero + 3hrs 15 mins starting point: Road forks BIENCOURT (Q.7.a.8.2.) via BIEFVILLERS to FREMICOURT. Received 74th & 75th Brigade schemes for operations. Forward areas. Submitted 75th F.A. Scheme for evacuation of Brigades in case of assault. Attack. R.W.G. Warning order on 12th August 74th Inf. Brigade to FREMICOURT as a Reserve Batt. 75th 7th R.W. Qrd? to FREMICOURT R.W.G. order No. 120, 75th F.Amb. to FREMICOURT I.26.b.56.	
I.27.b.	12/3/18		Marches at 9.30 a.m. & arrived at I.22.b. at 10.30 a.m. Moved on up to I.27.b.7.1. (C.O.'s N. 237/13.)	

WAR DIARY or INTELLIGENCE SUMMARY

Army Form C. 2118.

76th Fd. Amb.

Place	Date	Hour	Summary of Events and Information	Remarks and references to Appendices
T.27.b. Map 51.e.	19/3/16		Received R.A.M.C. order 96/2/2, 25th Div. to relieve 6th Div. in left section TV Corps front, commencing on 20th inst. 7.A.M. to take over 3rd R.S.A. Pigmies from 17th Wilts by 7.8. A.M. Relief to be completed by 6 P.M. Addendum to R.A.M.C. order 96/2/2. Relief A.D.S. to be	
	20th		completed by 12 noon on the 21st. Heavy fire on front of Corps, especially towards left sector, back areas being heavily shelled. Further instructions asked for as regards move.	
	21st 5am		Warning order 25th Div. defence scheme to come into operation, 4 bearers sent to each Batt. D Krigsalle. Medical reliefs of units 6th Div in progress.	
	9.30pm		Heavy shelling all round Lake sidi Kharpul to L.H.E. + many casualties occurring locally, several horses hit in camp + some other Cmds waggons. O.Cs horses killed + 2 O.Rs + 2 mens Rs. his Bearers wounded. Remainder of horses moved to Essel road P.[?] put in trenches, except bearer parties which are busily employed.	

WAR DIARY or INTELLIGENCE SUMMARY

Army Form C. 2118.

75th Fd. Amb.

Place	Date	Hour	Summary of Events and Information	Remarks and references to Appendices
I.27.c. Map 57.C.	21/3/18	4.30 pm	Decided to move heavy transport back beyond FREMICOURT on main road & to form a Dressing Station in BEUGNY. The Brigade advanced at this time & the Dressing Station at BEUGNY was opened as an A.D.S. GREVILLERS being used as M.D.S. Two officers + parties of bearers formed advanced Dressing	
		6 pm	at I.24.a. in Sunken Rd & at the Bst-rt-racing at corner of MORCHIES ROAD. Got in contact with the Battalions. Ambulance Cars were sent up to the MORCHIES ROAD.	
BEUGNY	22nd	8 am	As the Battn. rallying period the men being heavily shelled the party that was sent to I.17.a.1.b. All casualties that got as far as R.A.P's at Battn. Hd.Qrs. were kept there.	
		10 am	O.C. 76th Fd. Amb. at this time asked assistance in bearing. 75th Fd. Amb. with one bearer Sec. "C" "A sec." & 2nd S.T. joined additional to their own Brigade, thus gave Squds of two stretcher bearers with 2 men from 76th Fd. Amb. were sent to assist in this work arrived at BEUGNY about 7 p.m. About this time the A.D.S. at BEUGNY was heavily shelled & we had a few casualties caused by this, the enemy's artillery has the carried on in Gas Masks & prevented to his difficulties. As he and shelling continued all whis last Divisi. Arranged to tell some transport to come up to L.O.C.H. Camp + rendered assistance to 77 Fd. Amb. at the walking wounded station there.	
		11 am	A.D.M.S. visited the A.D.S. BEUGNY & approved the arrangements.	

WAR DIARY or INTELLIGENCE SUMMARY

Army Form C. 2118.

Place	Date	Hour	Summary of Events and Information	Remarks and references to Appendices
BEUGNY		4 pm	There was an attack on the front with a very heavy barrage extending as far as an beyond BEUGNY - The Bechtel factory has to be evacuated & cars sent from beyond BEUGNY.	
			At 5 p.m. I took all available bearers under Major d'Othman up to the R.A.P's & cleared all away at this time (the lads were just returning after an attack on MURCHIES.	
	8 pm		Captain Halton R. Harris, M.O. G.H.L. North Lancs reported at BEUGNY with 16 other stretcher bearers he has left, these were enquiries of where Naval Brig. Captain (Karslow) who managed under enemy night to evacuate many of this wounded.	
	2.3"		Cases came in pretty rapidly all night & evacuation was satisfactory cases were set from 2.5/19th 6th, 251st Divisions. Some units of the Divisions were relieved & their ways kept with the remainder, 11 classes taken by G.H.L. N. Lancs & Stretcher bearers.	
	10 am		Went to BEUGNY to relieve Captain Stephen who has been out on night having been continuous at work since first attack	
	12 noon		The horse transport was sent from Locq Camp to Front - on the PERONNE Road about 3 kilos from BEPAUME. proposed as was retiring to sink roads about BEUGNY some were still coming in from Bechuling & the pages. The night the dressing station was being shelled as the shells had to be evacuated & a dug out used for dressing patients.	

Army Form C. 2118.

WAR DIARY
or
INTELLIGENCE SUMMARY.
(Erase heading not required.)

76th F. Ambulance

Instructions regarding War Diaries and Intelligence Summaries are contained in F. S. Regs., Part II. and the Staff Manual respectively. Title pages will be prepared in manuscript.

Place	Date	Hour	Summary of Events and Information	Remarks and references to Appendices
BEUGNY	23.3.18		4th Division keep a chain of posts parts of where our are now advancing with ours of 73rd & 75th F.A. They sent an Officer please to find in touch with them but as they were not brought back any news, except from the supposed HdQr in BEUGNY.	
		12.15 pm	Last news from 11th Cheshires & Laws arrived about this time. Captn Sullivan R.A.M.C. + an orderly went out to get in touch with the Lines + are they had retired ten a line about BEUGNY, it was decided to remove the A.D.S. to a point on the main road just beyond PREMICOURT.	
		12.30	Left BEUGNY & took up position beyond PREMICOURT.	
		3 pm.	Received orders to withdraw along with Brigade + reform at BIHUCOURT CHURCH. Took over huts in Savoy Camp.	
	24.3.18	8.30 pm.	Received transport to proceed to a point on GREVILLERS - IRLES Rd at MIRAUMONT to form a more dressing station there.	
			Marched about 1 from + took up position near MIRAUMONT Railway Station about 4 and dealt with casualties from the 4th also coming in from the Division. Reported that the position was available, having only the V.A.D. relay men & stretcher cases with transport.	

Army Form C. 2118.

WAR DIARY
or
INTELLIGENCE SUMMARY.
(Erase heading not required.)

Instructions regarding War Diaries and Intelligence Summaries are contained in F. S. Regs., Part II. and the Staff Manual respectively. Title pages will be prepared in manuscript.

Place	Date	Hour	Summary of Events and Information	Remarks and references to Appendices
MIRAUMONT	25/3/18	8 a.m.	Under orders A.D.M.S. formed M.D.S. to BAUCOURT. Stretcher cases & walking cases so far as possible but transport for walking cases. Ambulance cars did not come up. Sufficient numbers of stretchers came up to deal with cases. WALKERS had in due course but they were sent out of ration.	
BAUCOURT	25/3/18	2.30 p.m.	Received orders to retire via BEAUMONT HAMEL to BERTRANCOURT.	
BERTRANCOURT	26/3/18	a.m.	Arrived at BERTRANCOURT & pitched camp.	
	4 A.M.		Received orders to march to FONQUEVILLERS.	
FONQUEVILLERS	10.30 a.m.		Remained heavy transport to POMMIER & formed an assembly station at BIENVILLERS to can collecting stat- cases of HANNESCAMPS & got in touch with the 74th & 75th Brigade holding the ridge about ESSARTS.	
BIENVILLERS	27/3/18	1 a.m.	Received orders to march to COWIN via BIENVILLERS - SOUASTRE arrived at 6.30 a.m. & took up billets.	
	3 p.m.		Received orders to move to PUCHVILLERS, arrived at 10 P.M. pitched camp.	
PUCHVILLERS	28/3/18	6 a.m.	Received orders to march to St. LEGER arrived at hillets at 2 p.m. (the 3rd M.N.E.) was enough by this unit in France 1916 on the way to	

Army Form C. 2118.

WAR DIARY
or
INTELLIGENCE SUMMARY. 76th Field Ambulance

(Erase heading not required.)

Instructions regarding War Diaries and Intelligence Summaries are contained in F.S. Regs., Part II. and the Staff Manual respectively. Title pages will be prepared in manuscript.

Place	Date	Hour	Summary of Events and Information	Remarks and references to Appendices
St LEGER	20/3/18		All equipment is practically complete though many rifles missing. Their mask "Shell pipe" (broken & phosn.) had rivers (filled) by shell fire & one heavy draught horse wounded. 6 men wounded & 6 men missing. The men came through wonderfully well & performed the last hard marches in the best of spirits, their morale was that of men seeking to collect a return to the infantry men ordered to retire like theirs came down saving away their own.	
"	31/3/18	7pm	Moved to CANDAS to entrain for SOUTHE.	W.C. Davidson Lt.Col. R.A.M.C. O/C 76th Fd. Amb.

Confidential

Volume 31   April 1918

War Diary
1/5 Ambulance RAMC

Army Form C. 2118.

WAR DIARY
or
INTELLIGENCE SUMMARY. 75th Field Ambulance.
(Erase heading not required.)

Instructions regarding War Diaries and Intelligence Summaries are contained in F. S. Regs., Part II. and the Staff Manual respectively. Title pages will be prepared in manuscript.

Place	Date	Hour	Summary of Events and Information	Remarks and references to Appendices
BERTHICOURT	31/3 to 1/4/18		Marched at 7 p.m. on 31st to CANDAS entraining Station & entrained at 6.30 a.m. on 1/4/18 for CASTRE. Detrained at CASTRE at 4.30 p.m. & marched to WESTHOF dressing Station & took over from 75th Canadian Field Ambulance.	
WESTHOF	4/4/18		Received R.R.M.C. order No 124, 75th Field Ambulance to take over left sector of line from DOUVE River to U.23.b.4.8; A.D.S. the at UNDERHILL 7 ARM, relief to be completed by 4 pm 5th April. Relief completed, came from Divisional Reserve as Part of ACHILLES.	
"	5/4/18		75th Field Ambulance crews employed as follows:— Brigade D.R.S. at WESTHOF camp. Evacuating left sector of line one Brigade. Collecting sick from one Brigade out of line. Medical arrangements for Divisional Baths, Divisional Reinforcement Camp, Divisional Wing, R.E. & Army Artillery Batteries, Baths, Canteens, Observation Posts, tending Brigade Entrainments.	
"	9/4/18		Severe attack by Enemy South of ARMENTIERES. Orders received that line held by 75th Brigade to be extended to the left.	

WAR DIARY or INTELLIGENCE SUMMARY

Army Form C. 2118.

Place	Date	Hour	Summary of Events and Information	Remarks and references to Appendices
WESTHOF	10/4/15	9 am	Enemy opened a heavy attack involving the whole division front - tending to the Divisions on either side. Very heavy shell fire - the dressing station at UNDER HILL FARM was hit & the whole barn and destroyed, one man wounded & the motor Ambulance hit but not disabled, there was between 7 & 9 am. Major Sullivan R.A.M.C. who was in charge decided to move the car stand further back to a point on the PET.P.R. Pont road. The Reserve bearers went forward & cleared the R.A.P of the left (South Staffords), some wounds had to be left at the 1/1 Wilts R.A.P. as it was in the hands of the enemy, the M.O. Lt. EDENS M.O.R.Q. is missing, also 3 bearers 75th Field Ambulance who were clearing from there. The relay post at DEAD HORSE CORNER was cleared & wounded.	
		9 am	Relay posts of R.A.M.C. bearers formed at UNDER HILL FARM & HYDE PARK CORNER.	HOR
		11 am	All R.A.P.'s being kept clear at this time they were	

WAR DIARY or INTELLIGENCE SUMMARY

Army Form C. 2118.

Place	Date	Hour	Summary of Events and Information	Remarks and references to Appendices
WESTHOF	11am		Placed as follows 4th Staff at AVENUE FARM; 1st WILTS at St IVES Post Office; 10th CHESHIRES at HYDE PARK CORNER — One Officer 75th Field Amb at Relay Post on MESSINES ROAD. About 150 yds beyond HYDE PARK CORNER. M.D.S. PONT-de-ACHELLES.	
	7pm		M.D.S. formed at WESTHOF, Brig 75th & 77th 2.A.S. + PONT d'ACHILLES closed as it was exposed at this time to Machine Gun fire.	
"	11/4/18	6.35 am	Wounded all cleared from R.A.P.'s. As there seemed to be an attack developing on the front of the 75th Brigade the PETIT-PONT road seemed to be bad position for an A.D.S. in case of any retirement. Orders were issued to the Officer in charge that he must change his position to KANDIHAR FARM if any retirement of the infantry took place.	
"	11am		Post at Petit Pont road had to be evacuated. Dressings & equipment were moved to NEUVE EGLISE–WULVERGEM road; post at LINDENHOEK 2pm was warned at Same time. Officer i/Charge D'station & the Staff warned to fall back over hill 63.	11 am

Army Form C. 2118.

WAR DIARY
or
INTELLIGENCE SUMMARY. 75th 4th Fd. Amb.

(Erase heading not required.)

Place	Date	Hour	Summary of Events and Information	Remarks and references to Appendices
WEST HOT	11/6/16	2 pm	The M.O. 10th Cheshire Bt. still at HYDE PARK Corner & walking cases passing down this way to Self-amb. But is and Hill 63 down to M & N BM AR FARM along the WHITE GATES road.	
"		2.30	A Car station formed on WHITE GATES ROAD & lorry's working from in front of this.	
			An A.D.S. was formed on the KEMMEL ROAD at T.3.d.o.6. [?] always led to the NEUVE-EGLISE — DRANOUTRE road about ½ mile from NEUVE-EGLISE.	
"		3 pm	Orders were received to open an M.D.S. at HAEGEDOORNE.	
"		8 pm	M.D.S. opened at 8 p.m.	
A.D.S. DRANOUTRE ROAD T.4.d.o.6.	12/4/76 8 a.m.		The 7th Brigade was forming a camp-site battalion two miles behind line behind NEUVE-EGLISE.	
"		5.30 pm	The Brigade moved to a position on ASYLUM Hill behind DRANOUTRE. A.D.S. was moved from DRANOUTRE ROAD to CROIX-de-POPERINGHE + M.D.S. at HAEGEDOORNE Closed down + evacuated to C.C.S. by M.A.C. Cars.	
CROIX de POPERINGHE	13/6		7th Brigade went to reserve position behind NEUVE-EGLISE was TRAVELS YTROM HCipL15 - C.D.S. at KERSEBROWE. MDS moved at BERTHEN.	

Army Form C. 2118.

WAR DIARY
or
INTELLIGENCE SUMMARY.   7th Fld Ambce
(Erase heading not required.)

Place	Date	Hour	Summary of Events and Information	Remarks and references to Appendices
BERTHEN	14/4/18	8.15 p.m.	Withdrew forward car post at KERSEBROM + moved it into a relay post for carrying forward car post now at HAEGEBROM. M.D.S BERTHEN passed about 80 wounded through.	
"	15/4/18	6.15 p.m.	7th Brigade harness were back to vicinity of BERTHEN to bearers are withdrawn to BERTHEN M.D.S.	
"	16/4/18	12.30 a.m.	Received orders from A.D.M.S to move forthwith to a position on the MONT-de-RATS — GODEWAERSVELDE (Q.18.b.) sheet 27. Marched at 1.30am + arrived at position at 4.20 am. Got in touch with 7th Brigade HQrs. A.D.S at R.M.Q. 7.8. near BOESCHEPE.	
Q.18.b.	"	10 am	Marched to C.C.S site on GODEWAERSVELDE — BOESCHEPE rd where 76th Fd Ambce had their M.D.S.	
GODEWAERSVELDE	"	2 pm	7th Brigade received orders to take over Corps reserve line in front of MONT NOIR, bearer squads were attached to units and a car post + reserve bearers stations at a farm on the rd map sheet (R.23.b.) sheet 27).	
"	"	6.30 pm	Lt. KILLEN M.O. R.E. attached to 10th Cheshires moved S/the camps into British lines.	
"	17/4/18	3.30 pm	Bearers now stationed as follows one party with Dr. KILLEN in HQrs the trenches at WOLFHOEK.	1430

Army Form C. 2118.

WAR DIARY
or
INTELLIGENCE SUMMARY.   75th Field Amb.
(Erase heading not required.)

Place	Date	Hour	Summary of Events and Information	Remarks and references to Appendices
GODEWAERSVELDE	17/4/18	3.20 p.m.	One Lorry Lo relay with Captain Chamberlain M.O., M.G. Batt. at TRIGRE Ind. Gr's near the Mont-Noir Chalesau. 2nd Relay in sunk road near R.26.A. Car & reserve bearers in farm at R.23.b.6.9. Car relay post road junction R.17.e.3.8. All the area occupied by the brigade was very heavily bombarded from 8 a.m. to 6 p.m., causing a good few casualties,	
"	18/4/18	7 a.m.	though up to 12.30 midday there were only 14 stretcher cases. The Brigade has been withdrawn to B.5 SO HEFE area & bearers came to GODEWAERSVELDE.	
"	21/4/18		25th Division Fd. Artillery will move to area A.32.c – B.19.B. Field Ambulances to W.C.S. sites 7.11.A.	
7.11.a.	22/4/18		One section 75th F.A. to GODEWAERSVELDE to collect sick & wounded of Artillery; chargine of station found in School about Gr. 15.0 7.6 month. S.O. arrived.	
"	25/4/18		Received R.A.M.C. Order No.189 – Division to move forthwith to Subford. XXII Corps to an area North West of RENINGHELST. Marched at 5 p.m. and took up positions at RENINGHELST-VAMSTHER FARM & A.D.S. at on the RENINGHEIST-LA CLYTTE road.	held

Army Form C. 2118.

WAR DIARY
or
INTELLIGENCE SUMMARY.
(Erase heading not required.)

Instructions regarding War Diaries and Intelligence
Summaries are contained in F.S. Regs., Part II.
and the Staff Manual respectively. Title pages
will be prepared in manuscript.

Place	Date	Hour	Summary of Events and Information	Remarks and references to Appendices
VANSCHER C.21.C Central Sh. 28.	26/4/18		A relay post was established at LA CLYTTE & agreed places with the units. The Division counterattacked at 3 p.m. 7th Brigade on left, 74th Brigade on right & 75th in support, 49th Div on left & French Division on right. The 74th Brigade got as far as high ground in front of KEMMEL village, took a number of prisoners but had to retire to first position.	
"	27/4/18		As far as known all the wounded were got away. Section at GODEWAERSVELDE began dealing with wounded. 74th Brigade are holding the line between the French & 49th Division in front of LA CLYTTE. Captain McLeod in charge of forward post was killed & became one N.C.O. wounded.	
"	28/4/18		Apart from shelling especially of back areas this day was spent until evening when there was heavy shelling on both sides especially towards MONT ROUGE.	
"	29/4/18		A heavy attack commenced on the French front at MONT ROUGE about dawn & also on the Brigade to the left of the 25th Division. The Division was not attacked in the morning but heavy shelling.	10.20

Army Form C. 2118.

WAR DIARY
or
INTELLIGENCE SUMMARY.   75th Fd. Amb.
(Erase heading not required.)

Instructions regarding War Diaries and Intelligence Summaries are contained in F. S. Regs., Part II. and the Staff Manual respectively. Title pages will be prepared in manuscript.

Place	Date	Hour	Summary of Events and Information	Remarks and references to Appendices
VANSOHIER FARM	30/6/18		74th Inf. Brigade to take over the front line from a brigade of the 49th Division, in N.9.c and N.10.c. Relay bearer posts are kept as at present.	R.A.P. as in diary. Lt. Col. R.A.M.C. O.C. 75th Fd. Amb.

Confidential

Volume 32   May 1918

May '18

War Diary
Medical
75th F. Ambulance

Army Form C. 2118.

WAR DIARY
or
INTELLIGENCE SUMMARY.
(Erase heading not required.)

Instructions regarding War Diaries and Intelligence Summaries are contained in F.S. Regs., Part II. and the Staff Manual respectively. Title pages will be prepared in manuscript.

Place	Date	Hour	Summary of Events and Information	Remarks and references to Appendices
VANSOMER FARM.	1/5/18		Line of evacuation changed to OUDERDOM — HALLEBAST ROAD A.D.S. G.30.d.4.9, relay posts M.31.a. & M.32.c.; R.A.P. ambulances at HALLEBAST FARM. While 1st Sub-division was proceeding from DOZINGHEM to REMY Siding to report for duty, the M.D.S. REMY – 1 man killed – 20 wounded; also a H.D. horses & 1 rider. 67 Beaver Division were evacuated in the Line.	
"	2/5/18		Two Batts. of 74th Brigade to be relieved night of 2/3rd by a Brigade of 49th Division.	
"	3/5/18	7/pm	Bearers withdrawn from line except Advanced attaches of 9 L.N. Lancs, who are being withdrawn tonight. 49th Div. Hd. Amb. has taken over the relay posts.	
"	4/5/18	7 am.	Marches to transport lines north of STEENVOORDE.	
"	5/5/18	11 am.	Marches to le BELLEVUE area with Brigade. 25th Division leaves fires to IX Corps – 6 a.& 2 ench army, 74th Brigade	
BELLEVUE area	7/5/18 6/5/18		will entrain on 8th May. Entrains at- WEYENBURGH & left at 10.05 pm.	

Army Form C. 2118.

WAR DIARY
or
INTELLIGENCE SUMMARY.

(Erase heading not required.)

Instructions regarding War Diaries and Intelligence Summaries are contained in F. S. Regs., Part II. and the Staff Manual respectively. Title pages will be prepared in manuscript.

Place	Date	Hour	Summary of Events and Information	Remarks and references to Appendices
COULONGES	10/5/18		Arrived in Camp 11 a.m.	
"	22/5/18		The Division will move to Mt. MONTGNY-SUR-VESLE	see App. 23"
			75th Field Amb will move forth with to IGNY L'ABBAYE & open for reception French Sick by 7 p.m. (S & 2")	
"		6.30 a.m.	Lieut. Division & equipment are moving in an S.L.S. IGNY L'ABBAYE to take over part Mil. Hospital from the French Authorities.	
IGNY L'ABBAYE 23"		6.30 p.m.	Main body transport arrived here & took over billets in the GRANGE FARM.	
			About 170 cases received in Hospital.	
"	26"	8.30 p.m.	Recvd orders to march towards with Inevn. Div. 1 Adv. Party to join 76"Brigade at VANDEUIL & that no more was to go to MUSCORT. Messengers were sent at once. Met gas from shelling the town. Sent back part Mil. Way from B.[?] on route to ROMAINE. Arrived at MUSCORT at 6 a.m. & established A.D.S. there. Space being attached to Batt. Brigade took up a position S. of the AISNE from MN 24 to CONSEVREUX. About 1 p.m. the line gave on the Left flank.	

WAR DIARY or INTELLIGENCE SUMMARY

Army Form C. 2118.

Place	Date	Hour	Summary of Events and Information	Remarks and references to Appendices
27/4 MUSCOURT	27/4		Flank fire the enemy carrying a Sep from the left behind the A.D.S. Park, which fire escaped two square army by batteries were only. M. Another C.A.S. Party was formed near the MUSCOURT (to MAIN road) mile from the latter. The Pill brought (3 the wounded) retired in a S. Easterly direction & encounters this YENTELAY. The enemy continued to advance on left flank and machine guns could be encountered at ROMAIN village. Moved A.D.S. to ROMAIN at 8 p.m. Dressing station there were machine guns fire, had to be moved & C.O.S. at MONT NOTRE DAME, many saw had the carried for miles, as there were no cars. One car belonging to 75th F.A. was captured by the enemy at the above A.C.S., on the way through TISMES. The Brigade moved during the night & took up position N.W. of MONTIGNY. The A.D.S. was fired at a position first outside JONCHERY.	
28/4 – 28/5/17 LAGERY	28/5/17		A message was received from Bde. that the line was to the N.W. of MONTIGNY, that further information would be sent when Bn. H.Q. was located. No information was received as to Bde. Position. attaches till had to retreat. All wounded was picked up that could be reached including some C.O.S. sites at MONTIGNY. A Recce party was established to MONTIGNY, about 6.15am, but the village was not the use attack having commenced at the infantry retreating towards JONCHERY & VENTRE AUX	

Place	Date	Hour	Summary of Events and Information	Remarks and references to Appendices
LAGERY	28/5/18		The transport was ordered to move through VANDEUIL toward SERZY, the lorries getting behind the Bgly. were instructed as follows. 2 squads with M.O. 9th R.N.Z's, M.O. + 2 squads with 11th Lancs + 2 hours with 3 wheelers. The other two hours with wheelers had been dispatched as messengers but could not again find the units - it kept changing its position. There were 10 squads in reserve with two officers. Arrived at SERZY about midday. Picked up casualties + evacuated them to TRAMERY which was still taking cases. Moved to LAGERY + joined up with 3rd Batt. Wounded Regt + 9 L.N Lancs La Fère 11th Lancs.	
ADRQNY	29/5/18		Moved during night with 2 wounded to CHOUQY and then to PASSY. At 5 pm 2nd Wounded came up again 9 LNL + details 11th Lancs holding a line S of LHERY. A.D.S was established in huts on Rd from LHERY— VILLE-EN-TARDENOIS.	
CUISLE	30/5/18		During night moved A.D.S transport to CUISLE. No cars had returned in morning so left C.C.S. Brigade retired to VILLE-EN-TARDENOIS, all cars were carried by hand from CUISLE + from there onwards.	

Army Form C. 2118.

WAR DIARY
or
INTELLIGENCE SUMMARY.

(Erase heading not required.)

Place	Date	Hour	Summary of Events and Information	Remarks and references to Appendices
CUISLE	30/8		Motor Ambulance & M.A.C. cars.	
LA NEUVILLE	31/8		About 2.30 p.m. moved A.D.S. to LA NEUVILLE as Bde. Head. Same to CHAMWZY in the evening to NAPPES. March at 3 a.m. to LES HAIES & established A.D.S., Bde. in reserve in BOIS-de-COURTON.	
LES HAIES	1/9		Evacuation by Motor Ambulance thro' Bois-de-Courton to FLEURY thence by Car to M.D.S. (9th Division) at NANTEUIL — by Motor Ambulance direct to NANTEUIL.	

A. A. Donaldson
Lt. Col. R.A.M.C.
a/O 75th F.A.

No. 75-7-a.

WAR DIARY or INTELLIGENCE SUMMARY.

Army Form C. 2118.

75th "B" Field Ambulance

Place	Date	Hour	Summary of Events and Information	Remarks and references to Appendices
LES HAIES	6/6/18		The enemy attacked on the right of the Brigade front about 4 am. About 90 casualties passed through, there was a good deal of shell fire, but only very slight damage was seen, there were returned to duty.	
"	7/6/18		M.D.S. (9th Div. F.A.) moved from NANTEUIL to CHAMPILLON.	17.20
"	8/6/18		Ambulance cars of 76th & 77th Field Ambulances returned to their own units.	
"	16/6/18	7am	Handed over A.D.S. at LES HAIES & conformed at FLEURY to Italian Field Ambulance. Rear Division entrained at GERMAIN for FÈRE CHAMPENOISE. Head Quarters of Ambulance proceeded with the motor Ambulance cars to form the transport at BERGERES. The transport marched from BOURGAULT to BERGERES on the night of the 17th/18th.	14.40
BERGERES	"	5pm	Marched from BERGERES to ANGLUZELLES.	
ANGLUZELLES	19/6/18		Arrived at ANGLUZELLES 2 a.m. Look up billets & arranged to collect sick of 74th Infantry Brigade.	
"	21/6/18		Marched at 2 p.m. from St. Loup to join composite Brigade of 25th Division. Details attached to 7th, 8th, & 9th Divisions.	14.20
St. Loup	27/6/18		Received orders to take over support positions in front of DAMERY, transport marched to FROMENTIÈRES on 26th but returned on 27th as the Bosche's were repelled.	

H.H. Wickham Lt. Col. R.A.M.C.

Army Form C. 2118.

WAR DIARY
or
INTELLIGENCE SUMMARY. 75th 7. Ambulance.
(Erase heading not required.)

Vol 36

Place	Date	Hour	Summary of Events and Information	Remarks and references to Appendices
ST LOUP	2/8		Unit moves by march route to GOURGANÇON.	
GOURGANÇON	3/9/18		Unit moves by march route to MAILLY.	
MAILLY	4"		Unit entrains at MAILLY.	
PONT-REMY	5"		Unit detrains at PONT REMY train of advance party arrives 8.20am. remainder of 5 a/6am. & took up billets at HERCOURT.	
"	6"		Receives orders to entrain on 7th at PONT REMY to rejoin details of 25th Division	
TORCY	8"		Received orders to take over billets at TORCY to collect sick from units at TORCY — CRÉQUY — FRUGES.	
"	25"		On return from leave C.O. resumed duties of A/A.D.M.S. 25th Division. Details from O.C. 77th Field Ambulance, 4th Field Ambulance, detailed 2 Field Ambulances to dela.. with 16th Division. (77th Field Amb & ...)	
"	29"		Received orders from XVII Corps to proceed for duty with 16th Division. (77th Field Amb for detailed for this duty.)	

H.A.Davidson
Lt.Col.R.A.M.C. ©

2353 Wt. W2544/1454 700,000 5/15 D. D. & L. A.D.S.S./Forms/C. 2118.

VOLUME   MONTH ENDING AUGUST, 1918

WAR DIARY

—— MEDICAL ——

75 FIELD AMBULANCE

CONFIDENTIAL

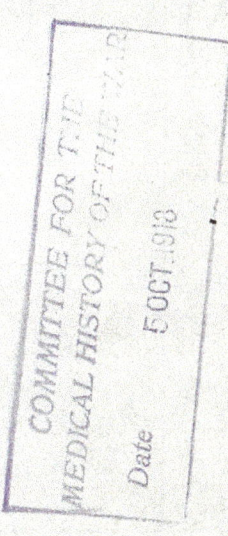

WAR DIARY
or
INTELLIGENCE SUMMARY. 75th Field Ambulance

Army Form C. 2118.

(Erase heading not required.)

Place	Date	Hour	Summary of Events and Information	Remarks and references to Appendices
TORCY	11/8/18		30 O.R.s R.A.M.C reinforcements arrived were posted as follows:- 75th F.A. 6, 76 " 16, 77 " 8	
"	13/8/18		Under orders of D.M.S. 1st Army & O.R's Tt. Hon.E. (Dental Mechanics) were transferred to No 3 Mobile Dental unit for duty.	
"	14/8/18		One Officer 75th Field Amb. 1 O.R's } returned from temporary 76 " 13 O.R.s } duty with 76th American Div. 77 " 13 O.R.s	
"	18/8/18		One Officer Lt.Col. W. TYRRELL D.S.O. R.A.M.C was ordered to report to D.D.M.S. ETAPLES for duty. Authority D.S.M.S. No D.9./94/13.	
"	19/8/18		One orderly sent to do temp. duty with No 40 squadron R.A.F. in Medical orderly. Dm.9 1st Army No P.L./853/153: 8.18.	
"	27/8/18		In accordance with orders of D.Dm.S RTH corps. One Lent Sub. dis.t two officers from 76 " F.A. Were sent to No 13 C.C.S. & 3 officers & 12 O.R's from 75 " F.A. " " 42 C.C.S. for temp.duty.	

Army Form C. 2118.

WAR DIARY
or
INTELLIGENCE SUMMARY. 75th Field Amb.
(Erase heading not required.)

Place	Date	Hour	Summary of Events and Information	Remarks and references to Appendices
TORCY	31/8		Lieut Sub. div. 76th Fld. Amb. returned to their unit. from No 15 C.C.S. Auth. D.Dm.S. wire No 67 of 30/8. Received notice that 77th Fld. Amb. was returning to the 25th Division from the 16th Division.	H Davidson Lt. Col. R.A.M.C. o.c. 75th Field Amb.

Volume 36   September 1918.

Confidential

War Diary

Medical

1/5th Field Ambulance
R.A.M.C.

Army Form C. 2118.

WAR DIARY
or
INTELLIGENCE SUMMARY. 75th 7th Amb.
(Erase heading not required.)

25th Div

Place	Date	Hour	Summary of Events and Information	Remarks and references to Appendices
TORCY	1.9.18		O.C. 77th Field Amb.ce reported Unit arrived at CREPY.	Keno
	2.9.18		Warning order for 77th F.A. to proceed by road to HAUDRICOURT on 9th (Prov. Army).	
			Captain a/Major S.D. LARGE reported to O/C 25th Div details + returns commenced of 76th Field Amb.ce (Auth. D.D.M.S. 1st Army No P. L/765/99)	
	3.9.18	11 am	O.C. 77 F.A. reported his details left for England on ordinary leave	
	4.9.18		Lt. DALY M.O.R.C U.S.A proceeded to England on ordinary leave.	
	5.9.18		Capt. MURRAY returned from Temp. duty at 1st Army Fench Mortar Sch.l.	
			Warning order for 76th F.A. to report to A.D.M.S. 9th Division (1st army 20248. Infantry 20248.	
	6.9.18		12 O.R's rein. proceeded for 76th F.A to 78, 6 & 76 , 2 to 77th.	
	7.9.18		O.P. 76th F.A. reported departure from EMERY.	
	8.9.18	10am	Warning order from 79th F.A. Div.ce to St RIQUIER Race (wire M202, 25 Div.W.A.8).	
			Proceeded to St. RIQUIER by lorry, transport by route-march.	
NEUF MOULIN	16.9.18	10 am	Transport arrived at St. RIQUIER.	
	17.9.18	2 pm	Handed over office files to A.D.M.S 2.S. Division	
			Units of 75 Fd. Amb. arrive 75 F.A. collecting sick from 25th Div.	
			Patrol's Carl Marshall NEUF MOULIN.	
			Captain CHANGE R.A.M.C taken on the strength of this unit.	
	18.9.18		Lt. HOWELL proceeded on T.O.B. duty to R.E. [...]	
	20.9.18			Keno

WAR DIARY
or
INTELLIGENCE SUMMARY.

(Erase heading not required.)

Army Form C. 2118.

75 F. Amb
or
9.5 Div.

Place	Date	Hour	Summary of Events and Information	Remarks and references to Appendices
NEUFMOULIN	23.9.18		Captain Change R.A.M.C. transferred to 76th F.A. along with 1 Sjt. 1 Cpl. & 8 O.Rs. 78 O.Rs. who had returned from leave.	
"	24.9.18		Warning order from 74th Bde. from move to HENNECOURT now.	
"	25.9.18		Transport with the exception of those vehicles proceeded by road to BUIRE. Lt. WELLS M.O.R.C. U.S.A. joined unit for duty. 11 cases of Influenza amongst men of 75th F.A. due to infection by two members returned from leave.	
BUIRE	27.9.18		Entrained at St. RIQUIER & detrained at ALBERT & took up billets at BUIRE. 4 M.O. and 8 Motor Ambulances at once detraining following situation.	
"	28.9.18		Div. Comes under XIII Corps IV Army. 8 more men evacuated with influenza.	
MARIBURT	29.9.18		Marches transferred to MARIBURT & assumed Opens. 6 more men of group evacuated with influenza.	

F.C. Davidson
Lt. Col. R.A.M.C.

Volume 37

WO 38

Confidential

War Diary

Medical Services

75ᵗʰ Field Ambulance

October 1918

Army Form C. 2118.

WAR DIARY
or
INTELLIGENCE SUMMARY. 75th Field Amb[?]

(Erase heading not required.)

Instructions regarding War Diaries and Intelligence Summaries are contained in F. S. Regs., Part II. and the Staff Manual respectively. Title pages will be prepared in manuscript.

Place	Date	Hour	Summary of Events and Information	Remarks and references to Appendices
MOISLAINS	1/10/18		Units billeted in MOISLAINS	
"	3/10/18		Received orders to march to the forward area. Marched under orders of 74th Inf. Brigade took up a position near the cross roads ROSIGNOL – HAPICOURT – RONY.	
"	4/10/18		74th Brigade in support – two Bns at MANUDROUFT – two of 74th Brigade in support of attack on LORMISSET Farm. Bearer squads moving up a quarter to the Battalions and an A.D.S. formed at Railway head near the GRANDCOURT – BONY road. Had a casualty for knee attack. 74th Brigade took over the line on the 12th and 1st Brigade moved into BEAUREVOIR.	
"	5/10/18		The M.D.S. was formed at Lt. TOMBOY – Ht. EMILIE road. By afternoon about 250 cases were found to pass through the M.D.S. All the R.A.P's were under medical handling Jas [?] … during the attack were kept there & were evacuated after the [?] … I went the [?] to [?] [?] from the [?] via front line, was left … [?] returned thru LEUZE WOOD – across [?] ... line advanced. Supplied by [?] Sand court farm via BEAUREVOIR.	
"	6/10/18			
"	7/10/18		Head Quarters [?] 10 moved to A.D.S. at Railway head in heavy banshell [?] to BONY. A.D.S. advanced beyond [?]	

WAR DIARY or INTELLIGENCE SUMMARY

Army Form C. 2118.

7.5.M. D.J.T.

(Erase heading not required.)

Place	Date	Hour	Summary of Events and Information	Remarks and references to Appendices
RAILWAY TRIANGLE GRANDCOURT	8/10/18		4th Brigade in Corps Reserve. 66th Division took over the line & attacked about 2 km to advance. A long way. Many wounded - 76 F.A. Advanced dressing station at Prémont opened.	
"	9/10/18	7 A.M.	Marched under Brigade orders. M.D.S. formed at PREMONT. A.D.S. at SERAIN 7 A.M. about 6 A.M. at 7.30 A.M. advanced to MARETZ with ambulance cars loading from 8 to 8.5 spearheads.	
"		1.30pm	A.D.S. taken forward to LE TROUX AUX SOLDATS. The advance was very rapid & the wounded not heavy. 10 cases found at Hotelip A.D.S. 2 squadrons of ammunition cars were found & captured. HONNECHY & BURTOIS.	
"	10/10/18	6 am	Advanced with the Hd. Qrs. 25th Regiment formed an A.D.S. at HONNECHY near the Railway Station taken over later at the railway BRIDGE R.E.O.C. R.A.P's in G. 26.9B. Walking wounded Dressing Station was formed at MARETZ where many transferred were stationed. Delivered M.D.S. at MARETZ 76 " F.A.	
"	11/10/18		C.R.S. moved to HONNECHY & had Ambulances posted in tens at G.19.2.8. R.A.P.s at G.19.d.2.4 & G.20.b.8.6.	

WAR DIARY or INTELLIGENCE SUMMARY

Army Form C. 2118.

75th Fd. Amb. C.F.A.

Place	Date	Hour	Summary of Events and Information	Remarks and references to Appendices
HENNEZEL	12/6/16		Received orders to march with 74th Inf. Bgde. to TREMONT at 2:30 p.m. Both Divs. relieved in the line by the 6th Div.	
"	13/6/16		Billets in TREMONT - influenza still prevalent amongst horses and a few new cases of mumps amongst the men. One Officer & 17 men & 3 horses left influenza. Left at M01S1A INSO with pri fever influenza.	
"	17/6/16		The Brigade was moved on 15th to Sub to MARETZ. 75th F.A. is responsible for all the 9 Sick wounded from 7th & 74th Brigades will be sent to near forty (?) hours attention. from 7th - 74 - 7th A C.M.R.S. have been formed near SERAIN. March'd to MARETZ took up S Q.	
"	18/6/16			
"	19/6/16 4:30 p.m.		March'd from MARETZ to HANNECOURT 7½ k. to right. The Brigade are in the line for 12 days. An A.D.S. formed in two places. A.D.S. for the 74th - MAUDDISE FARM Rect D Gr'd 5 v.v.	
"	20/6/16		Received orders to open a hospital for slight cases at Beaver Rds. ... 75 & 74 will use...	

WAR DIARY
or
INTELLIGENCE SUMMARY

Army Form C. 2118.

Place	Date	Hour	Summary of Events and Information	Remarks and references to Appendices
BENNECHY	26/10/18		76th M. Amb. responsible for clearing the forward area.	
"	27/10/18	10.1am	Bearer party under Captain Hughes M.C. with two horse Amb. wagons now proceed to point of clearing at Rest Sta S.E. of LE CATEAU – 26th Div. Surgeons Collecting post at BOIS L'EVEQUE – walked them line Bazuel – evac. to adv. dsg Stn 76 A. 3A	
LE CATEAU	24/10/18		Took up billets at Hospital at LE CATEAU (G.8.d.) Took over 1 Canadian Field Amb. duties 6th Division wounded to POMMEREUIL	
"	25/10/18		75th Field Amb. Bearers & 4 GS wagons took over duties 1 Canadian Field Amb. duties – MO Bearers Major J. STEPHENSON M.C. Heavy transport moved to BENIN	
"	25/10/18		Capt Hughes M.C. established A Collecting post at L 11 c 4.0 S 4.3 on 28th & cleared casualties of 74 Inf. Bde. E of FONTAINE. Evacuation through Yorks. POMMEREUIL	
"	28/10		80 patients in hospital, of which 59 are men of influenza. Hutted clothing & latrine arrangements put in order. No fight.	
"	29/10		No further cases of influenza received - the 19 men - sleeping car transferred to 77th (Ambulance)	

Army Form C. 2118.

WAR DIARY
or
INTELLIGENCE SUMMARY.

(Erase heading not required.)

Instructions regarding War Diaries and Intelligence Summaries are contained in F. S. Regs., Part II. and the Staff Manual respectively. Title pages will be prepared in manuscript.

Place	Date	Hour	Summary of Events and Information	Remarks and references to Appendices
LE CATEAU	31/19/18		74" Fd Amb relieved in the line. Capt Hoyle M.C. & party from Car Collecting post returned to H.p. Sgt Smythe & 10 of 74 Fd Amb located around LE CATEAU Station. New sick included & the rest. 252 cases of influenza have been admitted in the books during this month and in addition a large number have passed through to Corps Main Dressing Station & not retained.	

Stephenson
Major R.A.M.C.
O/C 74 Fd Amb

Volume

Confidential

WAR DIARY

MEDICAL SERVICES

75th Field Ambulance

November 1918

WAR DIARY
or
INTELLIGENCE SUMMARY

(Erase heading not required.)

Army Form C. 2118.

Instructions regarding War Diaries and Intelligence Summaries are contained in F. S. Regs., Part II. and the Staff Manual respectively. Title pages will be prepared in manuscript.

Place	Date	Hour	Summary of Events and Information	Remarks and references to Appendices
LE CATEAU	4/11/18		Two Sect. ambulances, ten officers proceeded to XVIII Corps Main Dressing Station for duty. Bearer Sub-divn under command of Capt Asst HUYCKE MC joined 74th Inf Bde. Sgnt B at MALGARNI, & cleared casualties of this Bde. Serving infantry resulting in the capture of LANDRECIES & advance beyond it. The party was put under command of Lt. Col. J.B. FAWNS together with all ambulances, cars, motor & horse. H.Q. out of action & remained in LE CATEAU.	
LANDRECIES	5/11/18		H.Q. moved up to LANDRECIES	
BOURSIES	8/11/28		H.Q. cleared LANDRECIES in morning & moved to BOURSIES. 74th Inf Bde Pers marched to BOURSIES in midst of division in the line & horse transport. Main Ambulance regained in convoy for day. HQ at 1500 hr.	
"	9-12		Personnel rested, equipment overhauled & pay cleared & wagons cleaned.	
LE CATEAU	13		Marched to LE CATEAU. Orders received to keep up 58 (?) motor amb. Cars not found daily by Corps & Army through in the district. Serving area of influence where a state of epidemic. Over 60 cases evacuated to C.C.S.	
"	14			

WAR DIARY or INTELLIGENCE SUMMARY

Army Form C. 2118.

Place	Date	Hour	Summary of Events and Information	Remarks and references to Appendices
LE CATEAU	18th		Lt. Col. N. A. DAVIDSON D.S.O. proceeded at 6 P.M. Dn on his appointment as Medic. of the division. Company command taken over by Capt T. STEPHENSON.	
"	19th		A.D.R.S. to. 50 patients spent up at 1400 hrs.	
"	24th		Capt K. Morany proceeded to rejoin 1st Div.in. Demp't Coy.	
"	26th		Reunion of duplicate moving by Pte Rob for Medic present. Lt Col. L. V. THURSTON D.S.O. assumed command of the unit.	
"	27th		Preliminary inspection of T.F.D. at 3 P.M.	
"	28th		Divisional Commander inspected unit. Graduated to thick to instructed. training recru. & ambulance from Bridge & Raine over No 66. Decided to A+CMES to take over filed from 19 h Div.	
"	29th		A tot of ambulance proceeded to STH NAME Lord LANCASTER proceeded to report.	
"	30th			

Volume 39   Confidential

War Diary

Medical Services

75th Field Ambulance

December, 1918

WAR DIARY
or
INTELLIGENCE SUMMARY.

(Erase heading not required.)

Army Form C. 2118.

Place	Date	Hour	Summary of Events and Information	Remarks and references to Appendices
ST HILAIRE	1/2/18		In billets. Nil to report.	
	2/2/18		Nil to report.	
	3/2/18		Nil to report.	
	4/2/18		Unit paraded at 1.30 p.m. to greet H.M. the King at 2.15. Arrangements made with Staff Captain to supply 20 men for Salvage Fray.	
	5/2/18		Nil to report.	
	6/2/18		Verbal instructions received from Adms. to open a Brig. Bath Station at AVESNES.	
	7/2/18		Advance Guard proceeded to AVESNES by march route to clean up hospital site. Adms. now received to the more AVESNES.	
	8/2/18		Unit moved at 9.45 to AVESNES. Unit provided 2 Offrs and Burying Commander if Stores booked the hospital to baths.	
AVESNES	9/2/18		D.S. Station opened at 11.40 am. Cases rec. evac. from 76th Field Ambulance.	

WAR DIARY or INTELLIGENCE SUMMARY

Army Form C. 2118.

Place	Date	Hour	Summary of Events and Information	Remarks and references to Appendices
AVESNES to AUBIGNY	10/3/18 to 11/3/18		Numbers at 12 noon. infants total 51. Teachers at 7 a.m. 48. Conference.	
	12/3/18		Teachers at 12 noon. Officers 1, Privates Sick 37, Influenza 1. Total So O Rs 1 Officer. Conference at Divis: Office att: Medical Officers.	
	13/3/18		Numbers in hospital 12 noon. 1 Officer 750 ORs. OC attended a meeting of Education Officers in Field.	
	14/3/18		Numbers admitted at 12 noon Officer 1. Pulmonary Sick 46. Influenza 11. Stations 5. Total 1 Officer 62 Other Ranks.	
	15/3/18		Numbers admitted in hospital 12 noon Officers 1. Privates Sick 48. Influenza 7. Stations 7.	
	16/3/18		Numbers admitted 12 noon. Officer 1. Notable 1. Aubigny Sick 48. Influenza 17. Stations 8.	
	17/3/18		Officers 1. Ordinary Rank 49. Influenza 8. Stations 8.	

WAR DIARY
or
INTELLIGENCE SUMMARY.

(Erase heading not required.)

Army Form C. 2118.

Place	Date	Hour	Summary of Events and Information	Remarks and references to Appendices
ATSGRÉS to ALBERT	18/12/18		Total Officers 1, Naturgick 44, Influenza 14, Scabies 12	
	19/12/18		Power left for Counties. Ambulances for interviews	
	20/12/18		In hospital 12 noon 57 OR 2 officers	
	21/12/18		In hospital 12 noon 57 OR 1 officer	
	22/12/18		In hospital 12 noon 49 OR 1 officer	
	23/12/18		In hospital noon 52 OR 1 officer	
	24/12/18		hom. 52 OR 1 officer in hospital	
	25/12/18		hom. 37 OR in hospital	
			Water G.O.C. inspected hospital. Who knows?	
	26/12/18		hom 39 OR	
	27/12/18		33 OR	
	28/12/18		hom 40 OR in hospital	
	29/12/18		hom 36 OR in hospital	
	30/12/18		hom 39 OR in hospital	
	31/12/18		hom 45 OR 1 officer in hospital	

M Murphy
D/ADMS Reserve

Volume

Confidential

25 DIV
Box 1999

WAR DIARY

MEDICAL SERVICES

75th Field Ambulance

January 1919

Army Form C. 2118

WAR DIARY
or
INTELLIGENCE SUMMARY.
(Erase heading not required.)

Instructions regarding War Diaries and Intelligence Summaries are contained in F. S. Regs., Part II. and the Staff Manual respectively. Title pages will be prepared in manuscript.

Place	Date	Hour	Summary of Events and Information	Remarks and references to Appendices
AVESNES les AUBERT	1/1/19		In hospital (non officers) Holiday Sick 23. Influenza 6. Scabies 9	
	2/1/19		In hospital none. Officers 1. O.Ranks 34.	
	3/1/19		In hospital (non officers) 2 O.R. 45	
	4/1/19		In hospital 37 O.R. Pte PRICE R.A.M.C. presented in.	
			General dewsbuchation to COMPANY.	
	5/1/19		In hospital none 38 O.Ranks. Lives known departed	
			Submitted.	
	6/1/19		In hospital none 40 O.Ranks. School opened at Methrophil.	
			Captain + Pte WALSH proceed to Clemitheati. Pte RALSTON proceed to dewsbuchation	
	7/1/19		In hospital 46 O.R. (none)	
	8/1/19		In hospital 38 O.R. (none)	
	9/1/19		In hospital 40 O.R. (none)	
	10/1/19		Two O.S. waggons sent to FONTAINE la TROOPE under Sergeant instructions	

WAR DIARY
or
INTELLIGENCE SUMMARY.
(Erase heading not required.)

Army Form C. 211

Place	Date	Hour	Summary of Events and Information	Remarks and references to Appendices
AVESNES les AUBERT	10/1/19		6 Ranks in hospital. now. 41.	
	11/1/19		O Ranks in hospital. now. 48 O.R?	
	13/1/19		S/Lark. S2 in hospital. Pte GOSBY & PTE WIGGLESWORTH left	
			to consolesalescene Friday	
	14/1/19		6 P. Rs 44 in hospital	
	14/1/19		O R's 49 in hospital. Cpl Marchand & Pte MAIDS? left & went to hosp.	
	16/1/19		O R's 47 now Pte S. enquirers the second in hospital at 11.09	
	17/4/19		O R's 35 (now) in hospital	
			Pte HATHERWAIDE. & B. OTHWELL to Convalescent	
	18/1/19		O R's 38 (now) in hospital. Ptes MOWATT. & to 4th Estaprs for Convalescent	
	19/1/19		O R's 41 (now) in hospital. Ptes NOODLESS. KILLAN. OMIT. RICHARDSON	
			PELHAM. MITCHAM. WALLER from	
	20/1/19		O R's 36 (now) in hospital.	

WAR DIARY
or
INTELLIGENCE SUMMARY.

Army Form C. 2118

Place	Date	Hour	Summary of Events and Information	Remarks and references to Appendices
ANZACS (3) AUBERT	21/1/19		In hospital S.R.S. 33 (noon) Cpl BARKER, Capts CRAMP'S OTES Boot GREEN LEES & LAMB Returned Duration Copland S.R.S.O's returned from leave	
	22/1/19		In hospital S.R's 27 (noon)	
	23/1/19		In hospital S.R's 37 (noon)	
	24/1/19		In hospital S.R's 39 (noon)	
	25/1/19		In hospital S.R's 41 (noon)	
	26/1/19		In hospital S.R's 40 (noon)	
	27/1/19		In hospital S.R's 39 (noon)	
	28/1/19		In hospital S.R's 42 (noon)	
	29/1/19		In hospital S.R's 42 (noon)	
	30/1/19		In hospital S.R's 36 (noon)	
	31/1/19		In hospital S.R's 38 (noon)	

3/2/19
W. Marriott
Lt Col
RAMC

VOLUME 41

CONFIDENTIAL

WAR DIARY

75th FIELD AMBULANCE

MEDICAL

FEBRUARY 1919

75TH FIELD AMB
WAR DIARY
INTELLIGENCE SUMMARY

Army Form C. 2118

Place	Date	Hour	Summary of Events and Information	Remarks and references to Appendices
AVESNES le AUBERT	1/2/18		In hospital ORs 38 (nom)	
	2/2/18		In hospital ORs 34 (nom)	
	3/2/18		In hospital ORs 35 (nom)	
	4/2/18		In hospital ORs 42 (nom)	
	5/2/18		In hospital ORs 42 (nom)	
	6/2/18		In hospital ORs 38 (nom)	
	7/2/18		In hospital ORs 38 (nom)	
	8/2/18		In hospital ORs 34 (nom)	L/Corp. Severino Raine left for demobilization
	9/2/18		In hospital ORs 42 (nom)	
	10/2/18		In hospital ORs 35 (nom)	
	11/2/18		In hospital ORs 41 (nom)	
	12/2/19		In hospital ORs 39 (nom)	
	13/2/19		In hospital ORs 37 (nom)	
	14/2/19		In hospital ORs 36 (nom)	
	15/2/19		In hospital ORs 29 (nom)	

www.ingramcontent.com/pod-product-compliance
Lightning Source LLC
Chambersburg PA
CBHW081403160426
43193CB00013B/2097